THE
SMART GUITAR
BOOK

Guitar Chords &
Scales Reference Book

Ian Visser

Order this book online at www.trafford.com
or email orders@trafford.com

Most Trafford titles are also available at major online book retailers.

Printed in the United States of America.

ISBN: 978-1-4669-5768-8 (sc)
ISBN: 978-1-4669-5769-5 (e)

Trafford rev. 04/29/2013

 www.trafford.com

North America & international
toll-free: 1 888 232 4444 (USA & Canada)
phone: 250 383 6864 ✦ fax: 812 355 4082

Index

How to use this book

1: What makes this book unique is the grid' pages that appears on many of the pages. The idea is to help us understand how chords and scales work. By cross referencing these pages we'll see how frets affect the name of scales, as well as how barre chords and power chords can be moved across the fretboard.

2: We'll also learn what transposing is, what chords work together in keys, and other exciting topics that will make your guitar playing experience a whole lot easier!

3: Learning to read the chord charts:

We'll do a quick study on how to play the chords, and also at the same time see how our unique grid system works. Let's start with how to play the chord C.

Step 1: Begin by placing your finger 1 on the 1st fret of the 2nd thinnest string, as in the diagram on the left. Note the position of your thumb. Make sure pushing the string with the tip of your finger.

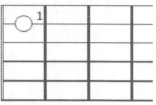

Step 2: Without moving finger1, add your middle finger, finger 2, and place it on string 4, fret 2. To test if the fingers are placed correctly, try strumming downwards from the 4th string. All notes should be clear, and no muted strings.

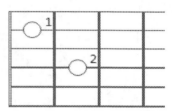

Lastly, add our ring finger, finger 3. this we place on the 5th string, fret 3. Our chord is complete. Try strumming the chord again, but now from the 5th string. Ensure all strings are sounding clearly, and there are no dull or muted strings.

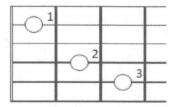

Some important facts:

3.1: On our fretting hand, our 1st finger is our 'pointing' finger, the middle finger is our 2nd finger, the ring finger is finger 3, and our pinky is finger 4.

3.2: What if we're left handed? Well if you're already playing left handed, simply replace the word "left" with the word "right", and vice versa.

4: First time left hand players:

Okay, if this is the 1st time, and you haven't yet bought a guitar, please consider getting a right handed instrument! You might want to know why? Here are the reasons:

4.1: We don't get left hand piano's, so why the need for a left hand guitar?

4.2: Both hands are needed to play guitar, both hand need to learn muscle motor skills. Unlike writing...

4.3: Left hand guitars are scarce, so your choices are limited, especially 2nd hand. Also keep in mind that if you want to jam on a friends guitar, it's more than likely going to be a right handed guitar!

4.4: The hand that you naturally have more control over (normally your right hand) is what makes you right handed. Now with guitar, your left hand arguably does more work changing chords and fretting notes in a scale. So, with this in mind, it's almost tempting to say that right handed players are actually playing the wrong way?

4.5: Are the results of lefties playing right good? Yes, I've several left handed students who began playing as a right handed guitarist. They've done really well. Again, we have to use both hands anyway, so in this instance I'd recommend rather playing right handed, no matter your natural preference.

5: The 3 basic types of guitar:

There are 3 basic types: 1) the **acoustic nylon string**, which is often referred to as a classical or a Spanish guitar. 2) the **acoustic steel string**, or folk guitar which it is sometimes called, and then 3) the **electric guitar** which relies on an amplifier.

The neck is wider than a steel string, making fretting easier. Note the difference in the head by the guitar tuners. This guitar is not as versatile as a steel string, but more suited for classical styles.

Steel string neck are more similar to electric guitars, being thinner than the nylon string guitar. The strings come in different gauges, thinner string set making it ideal for beginners.

Electric guitars are more expensive to start with, and of course the added expense of an amp. But, it is an easy guitar to play.

6: What guitar should we start with?

6.1: This is personal, and I'd encourage each individual to start on the type of guitar that they really enjoy the sound of most. There is a unnecessary belief that we should start on a cheap acoustic guitar - this is NOT the best, get the best you can afford, even an electric - unless you really enjoy the sound of a cheap nylon guitar!

6.2: I cannot stress the importance of being motivated to play (especially with younger players), and this must start with your instrument. It's sort of like learning to play football with cheap tennis shoes - you're just not going to enjoy the practice. So please, unless your budget limits you, treat yourself (or your child if you're buying for them) to the instrument that they enjoy the most.

7: Tuning your guitar:

7.1: For the first time, I'd strongly advise you get some-one who knows how to tune the guitar to help you! Should you not know what to listen for, or understand the concepts of 'octaves' (to be discussed later) you might just snap a few strings! Or have a guitar sounding like a warped banjo made from plastic.

7.2: Should you be unfortunate not to have some-one to help you, please try and include an electronic tuner in your budget when buying a guitar. Then, remember to read the instructions! Also bear in mind that many multi-effect pedals include a guitar tuner - although this is more for electric guitar players.

 Clip-on tuners are possibly one of the cheapest and most accurate. It's portable, easy to use for both acoustic and electric guitars.

 This tuner is part of a multi-effect processor. It's great for electric guitars, and can be used for acoustic provided yours has a jack - a place to plug a lead in.

 The tuning fork. You have to make sure you have a quality fork, and then your ear needs to know what to listen for too. Not a personal favorite.

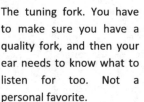 Pitch pipes are arguably the least easy to use, I've also found a few that are not too accurate. This is my least favorite.

8: What is "standard tuning"?

This is what most guitarists tune to. The notes as played by each string from high pitch (the thin E1 string) to low pitch (the thick E6 string) are reflected in the strings names! They are : 1E 2B 3G 4D 5A 6E.

Standard tuning:

Over the years many players have tried various tunings, we've listed a few here. Although some tunings allow some chord structures that would sometimes be impossible to play, the standard tuning is still most versitile.

Standard :
1E 2B 3G 4D 5A 6E

thin string   thick string

open G tuning

When we strum the open strings we hear the chord G. This tuning is one of Keith Richard's of "the Rolling Stones" tuning. It's also a favourite for slide guitar players.

open G :
1D 2B 3G 4D 5G 6D

thin string   thick string

open D tuning

The black Crows have composed some riffs that would incredibly difficult to play on standard tuning. Bob Dylan's album, "blood on the tracks" was one of the first albums to be recorded entirely in open D tuning. Also a great tuning for slide guitar.

open D :
1D 2A 3F# 4D 5A 6D

open E tuning

Songs like "it's so easy" by Gun N Roses, and also Jumpin' Jack Flash by Rolling Stones are great examples of open E tuning. Other famous guitarists like Billy Gibbons and Joe Walsh have also used this tuning which allows for easy barring of chords.

open E :
1E 2B 3G# 4E 5B 6E

open Em tuning

Another favourite tuning for Rolling Stones' guitarist, Keith Richards. Notice the only difference between this tuning and open E is the G & G#.

open Em :
1E 2B 3G 4E 5B 6E

open C tuning

Jimmy Page of led Zepplin uses open C in songs like "friends" and "Bron-yr-Aur". More modern bands like Soundgarden applied this tuning to songs like "Pretty noose" and "burden in my hand".

open C :
1E 2C 3G 4C 5G 6C

9: Detuning your guitar:

9.1: Many guitarists like to detune their guitar a 'half step', this means we lower all the notes by the equivalent of one fret. The best way to do this is to make sure your tuner has a chromatic function. Without this option we're restricted to standard tuning only, and will have to rely on our ear.

9.2: By detuning your guitar we release tension on our guitar strings, this makes it easier to play, especially if we're using a heavier gauge string. In other words a thicker set of strings. The heavier strings offer a slightly warmer tone and sustain, and the detuning allows us to play these strings with greater ease.

10: Drop D tuning:

10.1: This method of tuning is becoming a favorite amongst hard rock and heavy metal guitarists as it allows us to play really fast power chord riffs while only using one finger! To tune to drop D, simply detune the 6E string down to the note D. You can use the 4D string as a reference, but bear in mind that the 6th string must be an octave lower!

10.2: Once your guitar is in drop D tuning, all your power chords, called '5th's, will only need you to place your finger across one fret. But, should you wish to play power chords from the A5 string, you will have to refer back to the normal conventional power chords shapes.

11: Basic chord Dictionary – pg1

The purpose of these two pages are to serve as a reference for some of the more common chords that we might come across while playing most contemporary songs. Please do not learn them all, rather work on a 'need to know' basis. *Please keep in mind that the highlighted grey dot is the root note of the chord – not necessarily the bass note!.*

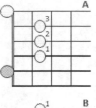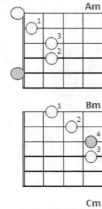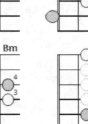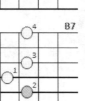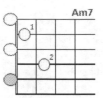

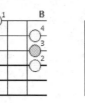

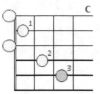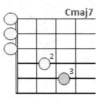

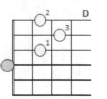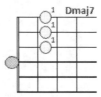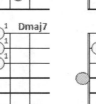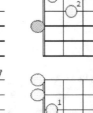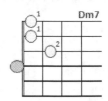

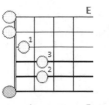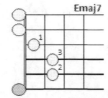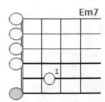

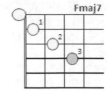

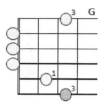 G
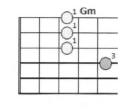 Gm
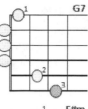 Gmaj7
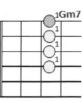 G7
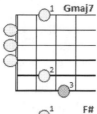 Gm7

 Bb
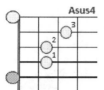 Bbm
 F#
 F#m
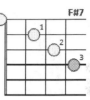 F#7

 Asus2
 Asus4
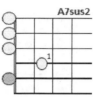 A7sus4
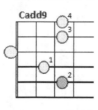 A7sus2
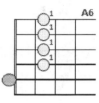 A6

 B6
 Bm7b5
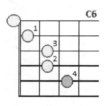 C6
 Cadd9
 C9

 Dsus2
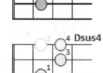 Dsus4
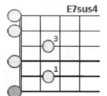 E7sus4
 Em11
 Em7

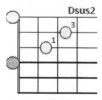 Fadd9
 G
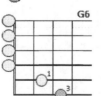 G6
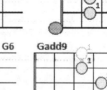 G6
 Gadd9

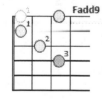

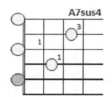

7

12: Inversions – a short introduction:

When we have a chord where the bass note is not the root note (note from which the chord is built) we call it an inversion. Here is a list of the more commonly used inversions. The original chord is written on the left of the 'forward slash', the new bass note is the note to the right. For example Am/G is an Am chord with a G note as it's bass.

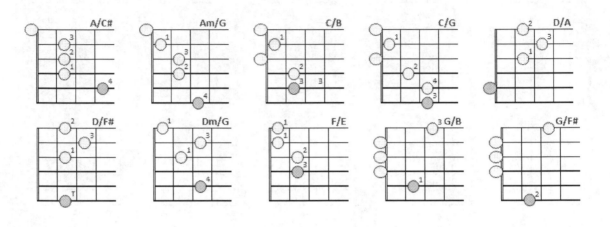

13: How to play Barre chords – root on the E string:

Barre chords derive their name from the 1st finger 'barring' all 6 strings at the same time while the other fingers fret the chord. Our chord is then 'moved' up or down the guitar neck. The full name of the chord is determined by a combination of the 1st finger position and the chord shape being fretted.

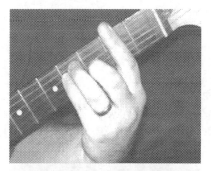

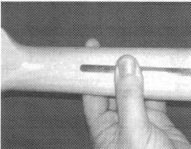

13.1: Please observe the 1st finger fretting all 6 strings while the finger is almost parallel to the frets. We also need to bend our wrist to get the 1st finger as straight as possible. Our thumbs position should be behind the neck, approximately halfway. The remaining fingers should bend around enough to ensure the strings are fretted with the tips of the fingers.

13.2: The chord being fretted here is the Major shape - see following page. As it is being fretted in fret 2, we have the chord F# major, which we simply call 'F#'. If we lifted the middle finger it would become F#m.

13.3: From behind we can see how the thumb is positioned. If we have it too high, we'll find our 1st finger bending slightly, similarly if we lower the thumb too much, the 1st finger could lift from the thinner strings. Not to mention the wrist might cramp unnecessary.

13.4: The **E shape barre chord** and it's variants get it's name from the normal open E chord shape, we need to see the resemblance between the two. To appreciate the similarity, try the following:

13.5: Play the normal open E chord using fingers 1, 2 & 3. Then replace finger 3 with the pinky, replace finger 2 with your 3rd finger and lastly replace finger 1 with finger 2. You should now have your 1st finger free. Your new chord is still E, just played with different fingers.

13.6: The next step is to move all your fretted fingers up by one fret, then bring your free 1st finger across 6 strings to barre the 1st fret. This means our 1st finger is sort of 'replacing' your nut, but at fret 1. This means we're playing the chord F. To confirm this, use the grid reference system as provided by this book.

13.7: If we go one fret higher, so that your 1st finger is in fret 2, we should end up with the chord shown in the picture above. This is F#.

13.8: Now from positions to the chord shapes as on the following page. If we're to remove our middle finger, we change from major to minor, or if removed finger 4 first, we'd have the 7th shape.

13.9: The key to using the barre chords effectively is to combine the positions (fret numbers) with the chords shapes, which are the types of chords. For example, if we need to play the chord Cm7, we'd first find the note C at fret 8. So we 'position' our 1st finger in fret 8, then we play the shape as shown at the bottom left of the following page.

Barre chords shapes – root on E6 string

This chord voicing, or method of playing a chord gets it's name from barring our 1st finger across all 6 strings.

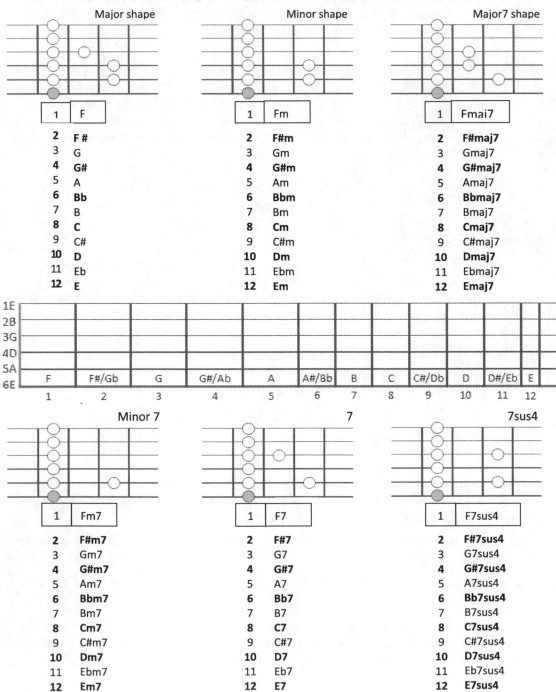

Major shape		Minor shape		Major7 shape	
1	F	**1**	Fm	**1**	Fmai7
2	**F #**	**2**	**F#m**	**2**	**F#maj7**
3	G	3	Gm	3	Gmaj7
4	**G#**	**4**	**G#m**	**4**	**G#maj7**
5	A	5	Am	5	Amaj7
6	**Bb**	**6**	**Bbm**	**6**	**Bbmaj7**
7	B	7	Bm	7	Bmaj7
8	**C**	**8**	**Cm**	**8**	**Cmaj7**
9	C#	9	C#m	9	C#maj7
10	**D**	**10**	**Dm**	**10**	**Dmaj7**
11	Eb	11	Ebm	11	Ebmaj7
12	**E**	**12**	**Em**	**12**	**Emaj7**

1E												
2B												
3G												
4D												
5A												
6E	F	F#/Gb	G	G#/Ab	A	A#/Bb	B	C	C#/Db	D	D#/Eb	E
	1	2	3	4	5	6	7	8	9	10	11	12

Minor 7		7		7sus4	
1	Fm7	**1**	F7	**1**	F7sus4
2	**F#m7**	**2**	**F#7**	**2**	**F#7sus4**
3	Gm7	3	G7	3	G7sus4
4	**G#m7**	**4**	**G#7**	**4**	**G#7sus4**
5	Am7	5	A7	5	A7sus4
6	**Bbm7**	**6**	**Bb7**	**6**	**Bb7sus4**
7	Bm7	7	B7	7	B7sus4
8	**Cm7**	**8**	**C7**	**8**	**C7sus4**
9	C#m7	9	C#7	9	C#7sus4
10	**Dm7**	**10**	**D7**	**10**	**D7sus4**
11	Ebm7	11	Eb7	11	Eb7sus4
12	**Em7**	**12**	**E7**	**12**	**E7sus4**

14: How to play Barre chords – root on the A string:

Barre chords derive their name from the 1st finger 'barring' all 6 strings at the same time while the other fingers fret the chord. Our chord is then 'moved' up or down the guitar neck. The full name of the chord is determined by a combination of the 1st finger position and the chord shape being fretted.

14.1: Please observe the 1st finger fretting all 6 strings while the finger is almost parallel to the frets. We also need to bend our wrist to get the 1st finger as straight possible. Our thumbs position should be behind the neck, approximately halfway. The remaining fingers should bend around enough to ensure the strings are fretted with the tips of the fingers.

14.2: The chord being fretted here is the Major shape - see the following page. As it is being fretted in fret 2, we have the chord B major, which we simply call 'B'. If we lifted the ring finger it would

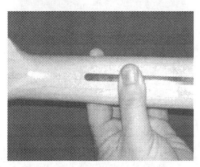

14.3: From behind we can see how the thumb is positioned. If we have it too high, we'll find our 1st finger bending slightly, similarly if we lower the thumb too much, the 1st finger could lift from the thinner strings. Not to mention the wrist might cramp unnecessary.

14.4: The **A shape barre chord** and it's variants get it's name from the normal open A chord shape, we need to see the resemblance between the two. To appreciate the similarity, try the following:

14.5: Play the normal open A chord using fingers 1, 2 & 3. Then replace finger 3 with the pinky, replace finger 2 with your 3rd finger and lastly replace finger 1 with finger 2. You should now have your 1st finger free. Your new chord is still A, just played with different fingers.

14.6: The next step is to move all your fretted fingers up by one fret, then bring your free 1st finger across 6 strings to barre the 1st fret. This means our 1st finger is sort of 'replacing' your nut, but at fret 1. This means we're playing the chord Bb. To confirm this, use the grid reference system as provided by this book.

14.7: If we go one fret higher, so that your 1st finger is in fret 2, we should end up with the chord shown in the picture above. This is B.

14.8: Now from positions to the chord shapes as on the following page. If we're to remove our middle finger, we change from major to minor, or if removed finger 4 first, we'd have the 7th shape.

14.9: The key to using the barre chords effectively is to combine the positions (fret numbers) with the chords shapes, which are the types of chords. For example, if we need to play the chord Cm7, we'd first find the note C at fret 3. So we 'position' our 1st finger in fret 3, then we play the shape as shown at the bottom left of the following page.

Barre chords shapes – root on A5 string:

This chord voicing, or method of playing a chord gets it's name from barring our 1st finger across all six strings.

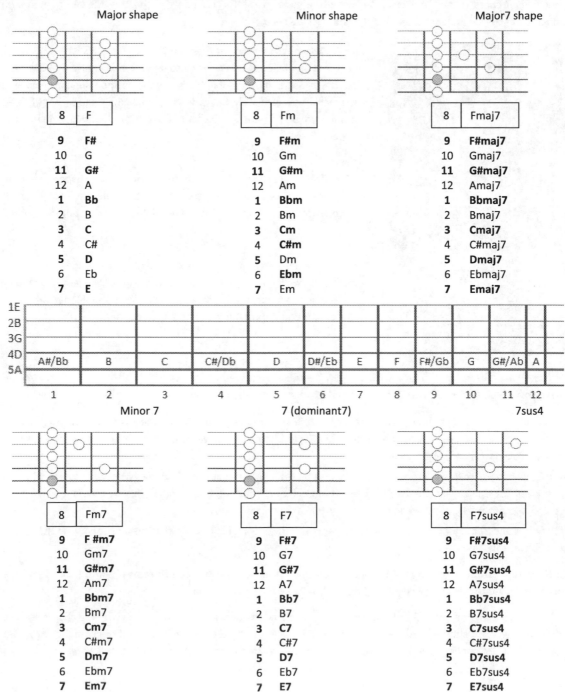

Major shape		Minor shape		Major7 shape	
8	F	8	Fm	8	Fmaj7
9	**F#**	**9**	**F#m**	**9**	**F#maj7**
10	G	10	Gm	10	Gmaj7
11	**G#**	**11**	**G#m**	**11**	**G#maj7**
12	A	12	Am	12	Amaj7
1	**Bb**	**1**	**Bbm**	**1**	**Bbmaj7**
2	B	2	Bm	2	Bmaj7
3	**C**	**3**	**Cm**	**3**	**Cmaj7**
4	C#	4	C#m	4	C#maj7
5	**D**	**5**	Dm	**5**	**Dmaj7**
6	Eb	6	Ebm	6	Ebmaj7
7	**E**	**7**	Em	**7**	**Emaj7**

	A#/Bb	B	C	C#/Db	D	D#/Eb	E	F	F#/Gb	G	G#/Ab	A
1E												
2B												
3G												
4D												
5A	1	2	3	4	5	6	7	8	9	10	11	12

Minor 7		7 (dominant7)		7sus4	
8	Fm7	8	F7	8	F7sus4
9	**F #m7**	**9**	**F#7**	**9**	**F#7sus4**
10	Gm7	10	G7	10	G7sus4
11	**G#m7**	**11**	**G#7**	**11**	**G#7sus4**
12	Am7	12	A7	12	A7sus4
1	**Bbm7**	**1**	**Bb7**	**1**	**Bb7sus4**
2	Bm7	2	B7	2	B7sus4
3	**Cm7**	**3**	**C7**	**3**	**C7sus4**
4	C#m7	4	C#7	4	C#7sus4
5	**Dm7**	**5**	**D7**	**5**	**D7sus4**
6	Ebm7	6	Eb7	6	Eb7sus4
7	**Em7**	**7**	**E7**	**7**	**E7sus4**

15: Power chords – basic theory:

15.1: These chords are a must for all rock, hard rock and metal guitarists. The chords are recognized by the '5' that follows note name. ie: an A power chord is written 'A5', and a C power chord is written C5.

15.2: To best appreciate power chords we need an electric guitar with a form of overdrive or distortion at our disposal. But, power chords also work well on acoustic guitar too.

15.3: Power chords get their name as they use the 5th note along with the root note. So power chords only have 2 different notes. Although sometimes we play 3 or even 4 strings, the power chord only has 2 different notes.

15.4: There are 3 ways to fret basic 5th power chord shapes using the root note on the 6th & 5th string. In these pics we've fretted from the 5A string, to fret them from the 6E string, simply move all your fingers up one string.

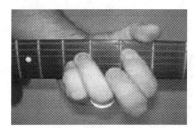  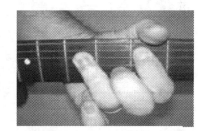

15.4.1: Above we see that fingers 1, 3 & 4 are used to fret the power chord. The middle finger is not used.

15.4.2: In this voicing, we flatten our 4th finger (pinky) across both strings. It's okay to touch other strings as we're only strum the root note, and the 1 or 2 strings below it.

15.4.3: We could replace the pinky with the 3rd finger (ring finger). Once more, it's okay to touch the other strings that are not being strummed.

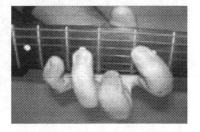

15.5: Due to the (standard) tuning of the guitar, we'll notice that the 3G string does not have the same note at fret 5 as the name of the open 2B string below it! In other words we do not find the note B at fret 5 of the 3G string. We find the note B at fret 4 of the 3G string. To compensate for this we have to include the pinky as shown in the foto. This is only necessary if we want to include the octave.

Other types of power chords:

Although the most commonly used type of power chord is the 5th, we get many other types too. Each gets it's name from the position of the 2nd note with respect to the root note.

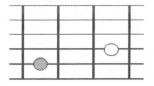

5th : The basic power chord as shown here. It uses 1st and 5th notes of the major scale.

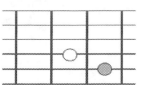

3rd : Also known as the 'major 3rd' as it uses notes 1 & 3 of the major scale.

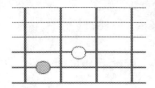 **b5th :** This uses the 1st and b5th notes of major scale. The 'b' is the symbol for 'flat'.

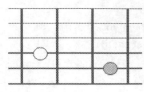 **m3 :** Also known as the 'minor 3rd' as it uses notes 1 & b3 of the major scale.

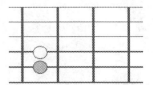 **4th :** The 4th, uses notes 1 & 4 of the major scale.

6th : Here we use the 1st & 6th notes of the major scale.

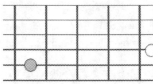

#5 : When we '#' (sharp) the 5th note and play it with the 1st, we get the #5.

7th : Lastly, the 7th, or dominant 7.

16: Applying the 5ths

We're only going to show how the 5th power chords work, to apply the other power chords on the following page, simply treat the root note the same way. The root note is the note indicated as the darker note on all our diagrams. The root note is the note from which a chord is built. It is often but not always the bass note too.

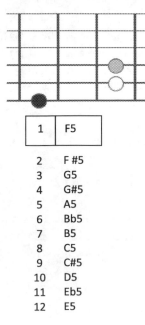

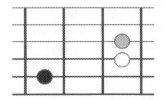

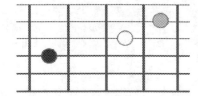

1	F5
2	F #5
3	G5
4	G#5
5	A5
6	Bb5
7	B5
8	C5
9	C#5
10	D5
11	Eb5
12	E5

1	Bb5
2	B5
3	C5
4	C#5
5	D5
6	Eb5
7	E5
8	F5
9	F#5
10	G5
11	G#5
12	A5

1	Eb5
2	E5
3	F5
4	F#5
5	G5
6	G#5
7	A5
8	Bb5
9	B5
10	C5
11	C#5
12	D5

17: Comparing the power chords to notes in the major scale:

17.1: Let's start by showing a 1 octave diagram of the major scale. We need to observe that the notes indicated by positions 6, 7 and 8 on the 4D string are the same as those on the G3 string.

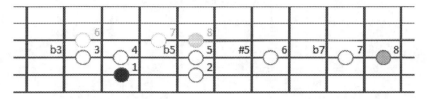

17.2: If we play the darker note (note1) and the lighter note (note8), we should realize that both notes sound the same.

17.3: The next step is to recognize the shape of the chord on the bottom left hand side. For example, if we play the 3 power chord, known as the major 3rd, we'd need to identify the highlighted notes in the diagram below left as the 1st and 3rd notes of the major scale.

Similarly, if we could recognize the 6 power chord uses the 1st and 6th notes of the major scale, below right.

18: What chords can we move?

There are certain chord voicings, or shapes that allow us to move them up the neck. The concept behind this is much like that of power chords and barre chords, the only difference is that we're not barring all 6 strings, and we don't include any non-fretted strings, or open strings.

Let's take the basic Amajor shape as shown below, diag1. then we move it up 1 fret, we now have the chord Bb in diag2, and if we move up one more fret, we have B, diag3.

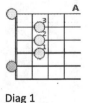

Diag 1   Diag 2   Diag 3

18.1: 17 notes per octave.

As 5 of the notes have 2 names, for example Bb & A# are actually the same, there are 17 possible names for the notes in one octave.

18.2: 612 chords to follow.

The following pages have 612 chords! To validate this, we have 36 shapes, and 17 possible names for them, depending on which fret and key we play them. 36shapes x 17positions = 612 chords.

19: Move-able chords, the triads:

19.1: Triads with root on 4D string:

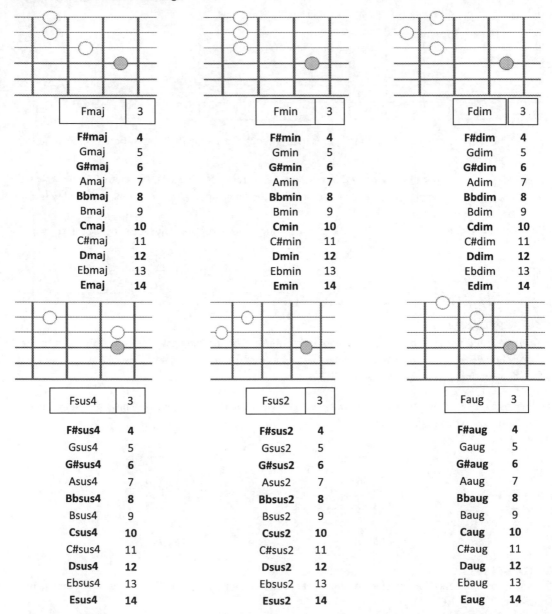

Fmaj	3

F#maj	**4**
Gmaj	5
G#maj	**6**
Amaj	7
Bbmaj	**8**
Bmaj	9
Cmaj	**10**
C#maj	11
Dmaj	**12**
Ebmaj	13
Emaj	**14**

Fmin	3

F#min	**4**
Gmin	5
G#min	**6**
Amin	7
Bbmin	**8**
Bmin	9
Cmin	**10**
C#min	11
Dmin	**12**
Ebmin	13
Emin	**14**

Fdim	3

F#dim	**4**
Gdim	5
G#dim	**6**
Adim	7
Bbdim	**8**
Bdim	9
Cdim	**10**
C#dim	11
Ddim	**12**
Ebdim	13
Edim	**14**

Fsus4	3

F#sus4	**4**
Gsus4	5
G#sus4	**6**
Asus4	7
Bbsus4	**8**
Bsus4	9
Csus4	**10**
C#sus4	11
Dsus4	**12**
Ebsus4	13
Esus4	**14**

Fsus2	3

F#sus2	**4**
Gsus2	5
G#sus2	**6**
Asus2	7
Bbsus2	**8**
Bsus2	9
Csus2	**10**
C#sus2	11
Dsus2	**12**
Ebsus2	13
Esus2	**14**

Faug	3

F#aug	**4**
Gaug	5
G#aug	**6**
Aaug	7
Bbaug	**8**
Baug	9
Caug	**10**
C#aug	11
Daug	**12**
Ebaug	13
Eaug	**14**

Please observe that the numbers to the right of the chord name are fret numbers. These fret numbers are to line up with the dark note. For example, if we play Amaj 7, (top left diagram) the dark note is to be in fret7. Similarly C#aug (above right) must have it's dark dot in fret 11.

19.2: Triads with root on 3G string:

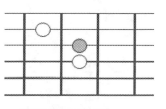

Amaj	2

Bbmaj	**3**
Bmaj	4
Cmaj	**5**
C#maj	6
Dmaj	**7**
Ebmaj	8
Emaj	**9**
Fmaj	10
F#maj	**11**
Gmaj	12
G#maj	**13**

Amin	2

Bbmin	**3**
Bmin	4
Cmin	**5**
C#min	6
Dmin	**7**
Ebmin	8
Emin	**9**
Fmin	10
F#min	**11**
Gmin	12
G#min	**13**

Adim	2

Bbdim	**3**
Bdim	4
Cdim	**5**
C#dim	6
Ddim	**7**
Ebdim	8
Edim	**9**
Fdim	10
F#dim	**11**
Gdim	12
G#dim	**13**

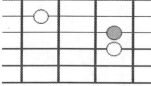

Asus2	2

Bbsus2	**3**
Bsus2	4
Csus2	**5**
C#sus2	6
Dsus2	**7**
Ebsus2	8
Esus2	**9**
Fsus2	10
F#sus2	**11**
Gsus2	12
G#sus2	**13**

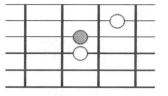

Asus4	2

Bbsus4	**3**
Bsus4	4
Csus4	**5**
C#sus4	6
Dsus4	**7**
Ebsus4	8
Esus4	**9**
Fsus4	10
F#sus4	**11**
Gsus4	12
G#sus4	**13**

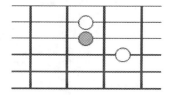

Aaug	2

Bbaug	**3**
Baug	4
Caug	**5**
C#aug	6
Daug	**7**
Ebaug	8
Eaug	**9**
Faug	10
F#aug	**11**
Gaug	12
G#aug	**13**

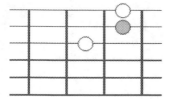

Dmaj	3
Ebmaj	**4**
Emaj	5
Fmaj	**6**
F#maj	7
Gmaj	**8**
G#maj	9
Amaj	**10**
Bbmaj	11
Bmaj	**12**
Cmaj	13
C#maj	**2**

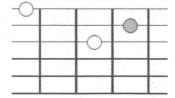

Dmin	3
Ebmin	**4**
Emin	5
Fmin	**6**
F#min	7
Gmin	**8**
G#min	9
Amin	**10**
Bbmin	11
Bmin	**12**
Cmin	13
C#min	**2**

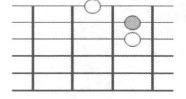

Ddim	3
Ebdim	**4**
Edim	5
Fdim	**6**
F#dim	7
Gdim	**8**
G#dim	9
Adim	**10**
Bbdim	11
Bdim	**12**
Cdim	13
C#dim	**2**

Dsus4	3
Ebsus4	**4**
Esus4	5
Fsus4	**6**
F#sus4	7
Gsus4	**8**
G#sus4	9
Asus4	**10**
Bbsus4	11
Bsus4	**12**
Csus4	13
C#sus4	**2**

Dsus2	3
Ebsus2	**4**
Esus2	5
Fsus2	**6**
F#sus2	7
Gsus2	**8**
G#sus2	9
Asus2	**10**
Bbsus2	11
Bsus2	**12**
Csus2	13
C#sus2	**2**

Daug	3
Ebaug	**4**
Eaug	5
Faug	**6**
F#aug	7
Gaug	**8**
G#aug	9
Aaug	**10**
Bbaug	11
Baug	**12**
Caug	13
C#aug	**2**

Note: We have listed the sus4 chords under the major, and the sus2 chords under the minor. This is done for comparison purposes. We need to realize that the suspended4th (sus4) chord is the major with the 3rd raised (#3), which means sharpened. When we raise the 3rd note, it ends up in the 4th's notes position. With the sus2 chord, we flatten the minor3rd (b3) so that it's the same as the 2nd note. With diminished chords, the 3rd and the 5th notes are flat (1 b3 b5), while the augmented chord has a #5. The root notes, or the notes from which the chords are built, are indicated in dark grey .

20: Chord theory for 7th, 9th, 11th & 13th

20.1: Major chords: Music theory dictates we build chords out of 3rd intervals, in other words we take every 3rd note of the major scale. To summarize, if we're in the key of Cmajor, the 3rd note up from C is E, and the 3rd note up from E is G, and so on. If we list the chords built we'd have the diagram on the right. The notes in the Cmajor scale : C D E F G A B C.

chord   notes in chord

C : 1 3 5 = C E G
Cmaj7 : 1 3 5 7 = C E G B
Cmaj9 : 1 3 5 7 9 = C E G B D
Cmaj11 : 1 3 5 7 9 11 = C E G B D F
Cmaj13 : 1 3 5 7 9 11 13 = C E G B D F A

20.2: When we get to minor chords, we need to know that the 3rd and 7th notes are flattened, with respect to the major scale. So our new list of chords are as follows. Please note that the lower case 'm' means minor. On occasion, we include a capital 'M', which means major.

Cm : 1 b3 5 = C Eb G
Cm7 : 1 b3 5 b7 = C Eb G Bb
Cm9 : 1 b3 5 b7 9 = C Eb G Bb D
Cm11 : 1 b3 5 b7 9 11 = C Eb G Bb D F
Cm13 : 1 b3 5 b7 9 11 13 = C Eb G Bb D F A

20.3: If we flatten the 7th note but still leave the 3rd 'natural' (in other words not flattened we get the dominant chord. A normal triad such as major or minor can not be dominant. The 7th note must be present. (See the section on mode theory) When we see a chord like C7, it means C'dominant'7, NOT Cmaj7, while the chord written simply as C, again means Cmajor!

C : 1 3 5 = C E G
C7 : 1 3 5 b7 = C E G Bb
C9 : 1 3 5 b7 9 = C E G Bb D
C11 : 1 3 5 b7 9 11 = C E G Bb D F
C13 : 1 3 5 b7 9 11 13 = C E G Bb D F A

Now there are a few other chords, here is a list of them. Remember, the numbers refer to the positions of the notes that are to be used, provided the root note of the chord and the major scale being used are the same!

20.4: **Suspended chords:** We get two, the sus2 and sus4 chords. The concept here is to not see the sus2 & sus4 as notes 2 & 4, but rather see the note in question as the 3rd note 'suspended' into the 2nd or 4th position. For example. If we're in the key of Cmaj and flatten the 3rd note we get Eb - this gives us the minor chord. But, if we flatten the note again, we get Ebb (E double flat) which is actually the note D, so we need to see the D as the E suspended into the 2nd notes position. Similarly, if we raise or # the 3rd note we have 3rd actually suspended into the 4th position.

Csus2 : 1 2 5 = C D G

Csus4 : 1 4 5 = C F G

20.5: **6th chords** : We get 2types, the maj6 or simply '6', and the min6. Their note positions are as follows

C6 : 1 3 5 6 = C E G A
Cm6 : 1 b3 5 6 = C Eb G A

20.6: **Rarely used chord types :** Here we combine major 3rd with b5, and a min triad with a natural, or the 'min maj7', their structure is as follows :

Cmaj b5 : 1 3 b5 = C E Gb
Cmin maj7 : 1 b3 5 7 = C Eb G B

20.8: How to use the previous chord chart.

20.7: A summary of chord types as often used in jazz, we need to realize that when we compare the 3 basic types of chords, these being major, dominant and minor, it's the 3rd and 7th notes that separate them. So we need these characteristic notes present when playing any of the chords listed here. Remember, our guitar has 6 strings, while the 13 chords have 7 notes! So this method allows us a practical method to fret the chord and not lose its essence. We need NOT fret the notes in bold !

maj7 : 1 3 **5** 7	min7 : 1 b3 **5** b7	7 : 1 3 5 b7	7sus2 : 1 2 **5** b7
maj9 : 1 3 5 7 9	min9 : 1 b3 **5** b7 9	9 : 1 3 5 b7 9	7sus4 : 1 4 **5** b7
maj11 : 1 3 **5** 7 9 11	min11 : 1 b3 **5** b7 **9** 11	11 : 1 3 5 b7 **9** 11	7#9 : 1 3 5 b7 #9
maj13 : 1 3 **5** 7 9 **11** 13	min13 : 1 b3 **5** b7 9 **11** 13	13 : 1 3 5 b7 9 **11** 13	7b9 : 1 3 5 b7 b9
add9 : 1 3 **5** 9	min add9 : 1 b3 **5** 9	m7b5 : 1 b3 b5 b7	dim7 : 1 b3 b5 bb7
add11 : 1 3 **5** 11	min add11 : 1 b3 **5** 11	7aug5 : 1 b3 #5 b7	Cmin maj7 : 1 b3 **5** 7
add13 : 1 3 **5** 9	min add13 : 1 b3 **5** 13	6/9 : 1 3 5 6 9	min6/9 : 1 b3 **5** 6 9

Let's assume we need to play the chord D11, we'd look at the '11' type of chord and notice the note positions are 1 3 b7 & 11. These are the positions of the notes in the Dmajor scale. The Dmajor scale has these notes :

```
Dmaj scale : D   E   F#  G   A   B   C#  D   E   F#  G   A   B   C#  D   (over 2 octaves)
             1   2   3   4   5   6   7   8   9   10  11  12  13  14  15
             D       F#              C               G     = these are the notes that make up the chord D11.
                                                           Remember that we must flatten the 7th note (b7)
```

```
Fmaj scale : F   G   A   Bb  C   D   E   F   G   A   Bb  C   D   E   F   (over 2 octaves)
             1   2   3   4   5   6   7   8   9   10  11  12  13  14  15
             F       Ab      Cb      Eb      = the notes required must have a flattened 3, b5 7 b7.
                                             This gives us the Fm7b5.
```

21: Move"Move-able" chords : various types of 7ths
21.1: Quartads with root note on the D4 string.

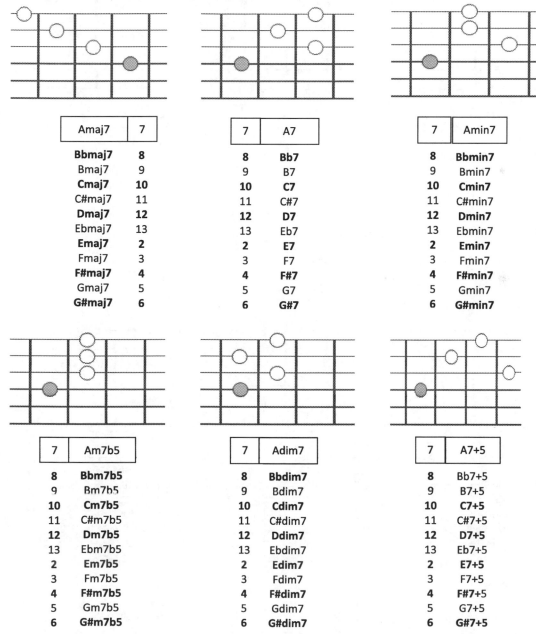

Amaj7	7
Bbmaj7	**8**
Bmaj7	9
Cmaj7	**10**
C#maj7	11
Dmaj7	**12**
Ebmaj7	13
Emaj7	**2**
Fmaj7	3
F#maj7	**4**
Gmaj7	5
G#maj7	**6**

7	A7
8	**Bb7**
9	B7
10	**C7**
11	C#7
12	**D7**
13	Eb7
2	**E7**
3	F7
4	**F#7**
5	G7
6	**G#7**

7	Amin7
8	**Bbmin7**
9	Bmin7
10	**Cmin7**
11	C#min7
12	**Dmin7**
13	Ebmin7
2	**Emin7**
3	Fmin7
4	**F#min7**
5	Gmin7
6	**G#min7**

7	Am7b5
8	**Bbm7b5**
9	Bm7b5
10	**Cm7b5**
11	C#m7b5
12	**Dm7b5**
13	Ebm7b5
2	**Em7b5**
3	Fm7b5
4	**F#m7b5**
5	Gm7b5
6	**G#m7b5**

7	Adim7
8	**Bbdim7**
9	Bdim7
10	**Cdim7**
11	C#dim7
12	**Ddim7**
13	Ebdim7
2	**Edim7**
3	Fdim7
4	**F#dim7**
5	Gdim7
6	**G#dim7**

7	A7+5
8	**Bb7+5**
9	B7+5
10	**C7+5**
11	C#7+5
12	**D7+5**
13	Eb7+5
2	**E7+5**
3	F7+5
4	**F#7+5**
5	G7+5
6	**G#7+5**

21.2: Quartads with the root note on 5A string:

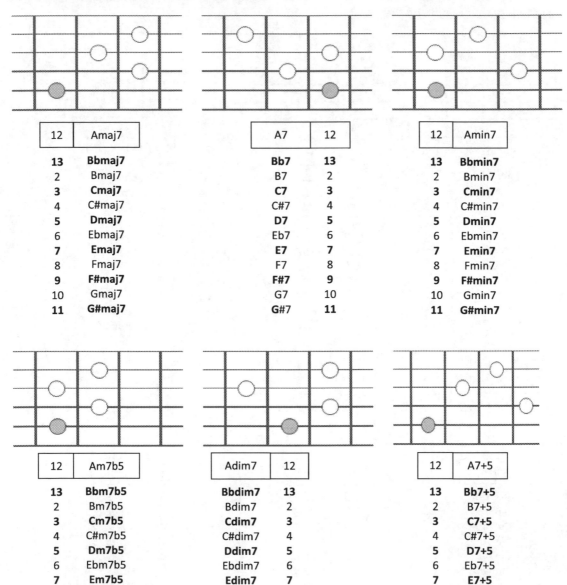

12	Amaj7

13	**Bbmaj7**
2	Bmaj7
3	**Cmaj7**
4	C#maj7
5	**Dmaj7**
6	Ebmaj7
7	**Emaj7**
8	Fmaj7
9	**F#maj7**
10	Gmaj7
11	**G#maj7**

A7	12

Bb7	**13**
B7	2
C7	**3**
C#7	4
D7	**5**
Eb7	6
E7	**7**
F7	8
F#7	**9**
G7	10
G#7	**11**

12	Amin7

13	**Bbmin7**
2	Bmin7
3	**Cmin7**
4	C#min7
5	**Dmin7**
6	Ebmin7
7	**Emin7**
8	Fmin7
9	**F#min7**
10	Gmin7
11	**G#min7**

12	Am7b5

13	**Bbm7b5**
2	Bm7b5
3	**Cm7b5**
4	C#m7b5
5	**Dm7b5**
6	Ebm7b5
7	**Em7b5**
8	Fm7b5
9	**F#m7b5**
10	Gm7b5
11	**G#m7b5**

Adim7	12

Bbdim7	**13**
Bdim7	2
Cdim7	**3**
C#dim7	4
Ddim7	**5**
Ebdim7	6
Edim7	**7**
Fdim7	8
F#dim7	**9**
Gdim7	10
G#dim7	**11**

12	A7+5

13	**Bb7+5**
2	B7+5
3	**C7+5**
4	C#7+5
5	**D7+5**
6	Eb7+5
7	**E7+5**
8	F7+5
9	**F#7+5**
10	G7+5
11	**G#7+5**

21.3: Quartads with root note on 6E string:

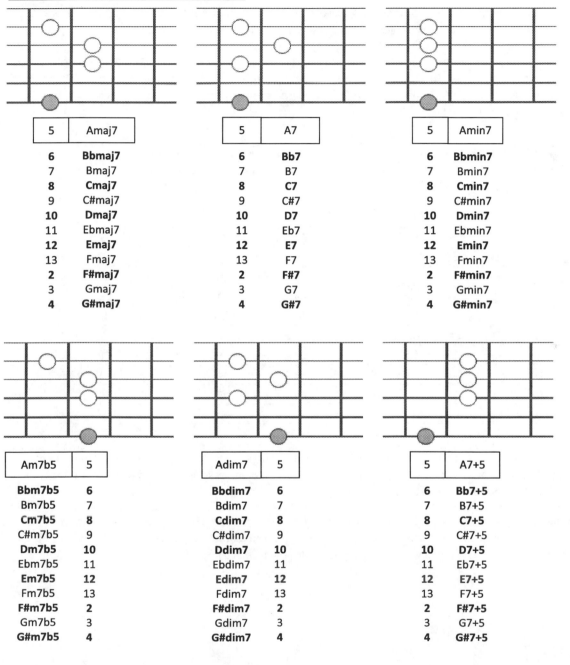

5	Amaj7
6	**Bbmaj7**
7	Bmaj7
8	**Cmaj7**
9	C#maj7
10	**Dmaj7**
11	Ebmaj7
12	**Emaj7**
13	Fmaj7
2	**F#maj7**
3	Gmaj7
4	**G#maj7**

5	A7
6	**Bb7**
7	B7
8	**C7**
9	C#7
10	**D7**
11	Eb7
12	**E7**
13	F7
2	**F#7**
3	G7
4	**G#7**

5	Amin7
6	**Bbmin7**
7	Bmin7
8	**Cmin7**
9	C#min7
10	**Dmin7**
11	Ebmin7
12	**Emin7**
13	Fmin7
2	**F#min7**
3	Gmin7
4	**G#min7**

Am7b5	5
Bbm7b5	6
Bm7b5	7
Cm7b5	8
C#m7b5	9
Dm7b5	10
Ebm7b5	11
Em7b5	12
Fm7b5	13
F#m7b5	2
Gm7b5	3
G#m7b5	4

Adim7	5
Bbdim7	6
Bdim7	7
Cdim7	8
C#dim7	9
Ddim7	10
Ebdim7	11
Edim7	12
Fdim7	13
F#dim7	2
Gdim7	3
G#dim7	4

5	A7+5
6	**Bb7+5**
7	B7+5
8	**C7+5**
9	C#7+5
10	**D7+5**
11	Eb7+5
12	**E7+5**
13	F7+5
2	**F#7+5**
3	G7+5
4	**G#7+5**

22: Using a capo

22.1: Capo's are perfect when you want the voicings of open chords, but in keys other than normally offered in standard tuning. They also allow you quick key changes if you need to transpose up in pitch.

22.2: If you wish to transpose up, simply put the capo at fret 1, 2, 3 or even as high as fret 8 (although this is rare), and continue to play the same shape chords. The idea is to treat the capo as you're guitars nut, then play the chord shape as if you're actually at the open position. For example, if you have your capo at fret 3, and you play the normal A shape, your fingers should be in the 5th fret.

22.3: Below we list the names of the chord implied should you use a capo at the fret number as indicated. For example, should you have played the chord shape A with the capo at fret 3, the chord implied is actually C.

open shape:	C	D	E	F	G	A	B	Bb	C#	Eb	F#	G#
Capo @ fret →												
1	C#	Eb	F	F#	G#	Bb	C	B	D	E	G	A
2	D	E	F#	G	A	B	C#	C	Eb	F	G#	Bb
3	Eb	F	G	G#	Bb	C	D	C#	E	F#	A	B
4	E	F#	G#	A	B	C#	Eb	D	F	G	Bb	C
5	F	G	A	Bb	C	D	E	Eb	F#	G#	B	C#
6	F#	G#	Bb	B	C#	Eb	F	E	G	A	C	D
7	G	A	B	C	D	E	F#	F	G#	Bb	C#	Eb
8	G#	Bb	C	C#	Eb	F	G	F#	A	B	D	E
9	A	B	C#	D	E	F#	G#	G	A#	C	Eb	F
10	Bb	C	D	Eb	F	G	A	G#	B	C#	E	F#

22.4: The first column of numbers represents the fret in which your capo would be position. The row to the right of each number will be the new name of the chords being played. For example, if your capo was at fret 2, and you played the chord D, the new chord is actually E.

22.5: Remember, if your chord was a minor chord, it must remain a minor chord. For example, if you played an Em chord, and now you have a capo at fret 4, you're now implying a G#m chord, so even though E becomes G# at fret 4, the type of chord remains the same. ("minor" being the type of chord)

22.6: Types of capos:

We get many types and designs of capo, here are a few of the more commonly used types.

The clamp type, possibly the most common type, easy to use and affordable.

This method might need some adjustments when using for more than one guitar. Not a favorite, but still works well.

A more recent design, very easy to use, and smaller so it does not hinder chords, but justifiably little more costly.

22.7: Not sure if a capo is for you?

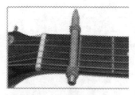

So you'd like to test the capo concept? Here's a quick method. Using a pencil and elastic, you can make a makeshift capo quite easily. Not an ideal for professional use, but at least you can test and see if the purchase of a capo will be ideal. Personally I'd suggest you have one, even though you might seldom use it.

Make sure that when using a capo, that all the strings can ring clearly when strummed unfretted - there must be no muted or damped notes. Also bear in mind that a capo will raise the pitch of the key you're in, not lower it! If you have a guitar with 'jumbo' (a type of fret)or large frets, please make sure that the capo does not the bend the strings out of tune! If you find your guitar sounds out-of-tune when using a capo, please consult your local music store.

23: Blank guitar TAB sheet – useful to photocopy

24: Notes on the guitar neck:

24.1: Below we've shown the notes on the guitar neck, assuming your guitar is in **standard** tuning. If you enjoy 'drop d' tuning, simply apply our grid reference system for your new adapted diagram. The purpose of this page is to show us where all the notes can be found.

Standard tuning :

	1	2	3	4	5	6	7	8	9	10	11	12	13	14	15
1E	F	F#/Gb	G	G#/Ab	A	A#/Bb	B	C	C#/Db	D	D#/Eb	E	F	F#/Gb	G
2B	C	C#/Db	D	D#/Eb	E	F	F#/Gb	G	G#/Ab	A	A#/Bb	B	C	C#/Db	D
3G	G#/Ab	A	A#/Bb	B	C	C#/Db	D	D#/Eb	E	F	F#/Gb	G	G#/Ab	A	A#/Bb
4D	D#/Eb	E	F	F#/Gb	G	G#/Ab	A	A#/Bb	B	C	C#/Db	D	D#/Eb	E	F
5A	A#/Bb	B	C	C#/Db	D	D#/Eb	E	F	F#/Gb	G	G#/Ab	A	A#/Bb	B	C
6E	F	F#/Gb	G	G#/Ab	A	A#/Bb	B	C	C#/Db	D	D#/Eb	E	F	F#/Gb	G
			3		5		7		9			12			15

24.2: And here we've shown the notes if you're in **'drop D'** tuning. Please observe that it's only the notes on the thickest E6 string that has changed. All that's really happened is that the notes have moved up 2 frets – for example the note G is now on fret 5, where-as with standard tuning G is at fret 3.

Drop D Tuning:

	1	2	3	4	5	6	7	8	9	10	11	12	13	14	15
1E	F	F#/Gb	G	G#/Ab	A	A#/Bb	B	C	C#/Db	D	D#/Eb	E	F	F#/Gb	G
2B	C	C#/Db	D	D#/Eb	E	F	F#/Gb	G	G#/Ab	A	A#/Bb	B	C	C#/Db	D
3G	G#/Ab	A	A#/Bb	B	C	C#/Db	D	D#/Eb	E	F	F#/Gb	G	G#/Ab	A	A#/Bb
4D	D#/Eb	E	F	F#/Gb	G	G#/Ab	A	A#/Bb	B	C	C#/Db	D	D#/Eb	E	F
5A	A#/Bb	B	C	C#/Db	D	D#/Eb	E	F	F#/Gb	G	G#/Ab	A	A#/Bb	B	C
6D	D#/Eb	E	F	F#/Gb	G	G#/Ab	A	A#/Bb	B	C	C#/Db	D	D#/Eb	E	F
			3		5		7		9			12			15

Note:

For acoustic steel string guitarists as well as electric players. Please notice the small dots on the top of your guitar, as well as the 'inlay's on your guitar neck. At frets 3, 5, 7, 9, & 15 we normally find a dot. While at fret 12 we have a double dot. This is to help us locate the frets quicker.

We also need to realize that at the 12th fret the notes begin to repeat themselves. In other words the notes at the 1st fret are the same as the notes at fret 13. Similarly fret 2 has the same notes as fret 14.

Now the notes from fret 12 are higher in pitch than those from open position, even though they have the same name. We say that these notes are an octave higher.

25: What is an octave?

An octave is a note that although it has the same note name as another, it is either higher in pitch (an octave up) or lower in pitch (an octave down)

For example, let's take the note G at fret 5 of the 4D string. (The 4th string from the thinnest). An octave higher in pitch can be found at fret8 of the 2B string, fret 12 of the 3G string and also fret 17 of the 4D string. While we can find it's lower octave at fret 3 of the 6E string. Lastly, the note G at fret 10 of the 5A string is the same pitch, it is NOT an octave.

Drop D tuning allows fast changes for power chords while only using 1 finger. This allows for very quick rhythms as favored by many heavy metal and hard rock guitarists.

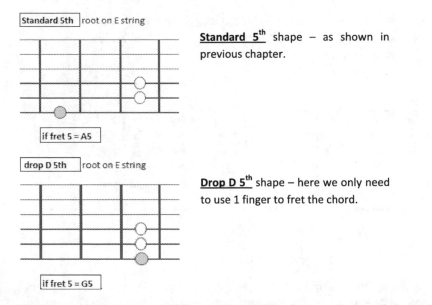

Standard 5th shape – as shown in previous chapter.

Drop D 5th shape – here we only need to use 1 finger to fret the chord.

Please know that only power chords using the E6 string as the root note will change their shape when drop-D tuning is used. All other chords and power chords will remain unaltered assuming the E6string is not in played.

27: Basic chord theory:

Definition of a chord: Two or more different notes played at the same time.

We're going to start with the most commonly used chords, like the major & minor chords. We refer to these chords as triads, as they contain 3 different notes. (Octaves are not regarded as different notes)

The rule for building a chord is to take every alternative note from a major scale. For example, if we wanted to build a Cmaj chord, we'd take the 1st, 3rd & 5th notes of the Cmajor scale. It'll look something like this:

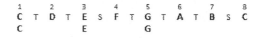

27.1: The notes, C E & G, are the 1st, 3rd & 5th notes of the Cmajor scale which make up the chord Cmajor, which we simply write as C.

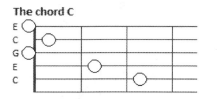

The chord C

27.2: Here we have the chord C, we can see that although there are 5 notes, there are only 3 different notes! All our basic major and minor chords are triads.

The next step is to build a chord from each of the 7 positions of the scale. For this we'll need to extend the scale.

1		2		3		4		5		6		7		8						
C	T	D	T	E	S	F	T	G	T	A	T	B	S	C	T	D	T	E	S	F
C		2T		E		$1^1/_2$T		G												

Now we include the intervals. There's a 2 tone interval from C to E, and a 11/2 tone interval from E to G. This sequence of intervals give us the major triad. So our chord is Cmajor.

D	$1^1/_2$T	F	2T	A		

Starting on the 2nd note, D, we first get a $1^1/_2$ tone interval from D to F, then a 2T interval from F to A. These intervals give us the minor triad. So our chord is Dmin triad.

| E | $1^1/_2$T | G | 2T | B |

The 3rd note, E, we get the same $1^1/_2$ tone interval from E to G, and a 2T interval from G to B. Once more we have a minor triad. Our chord is Eminor.

| F | 2T | A | $1^1/_2$T | C |

The 4th position, F, returns to 2 tone interval from F to A, and a 11/2 tone interval from A to C. Our chord is now Fmajor.

| G | 2T | B | $1^1/_2$T | D |

Position 5 has the same intervals as positions 1 & 4, we have build the chord Gmaj from our 5th note.

| A | $1^1/_2$T | C | 2T | E |

Position 6, has the minor chord's intervals, so here we build the chord Aminor.

27.3: Major vs minor triads. From the above method of working out chords, we can see that when there is a two tone (2T) interval from the 1st to the 3rd note and a one-and-a-half tone interval ($1^1/_2$T) interval from the 3rd to the 5th notes we get a major triad.

If we now reverse the sequence, in other words we have a one-and-a-half tone interval ($1^1/_2$T) interval from the 1st to the 3rd, and a two tone interval from the 3rd to the 5th notes we get a minor triad. The next step is to compare what happened to the 3rd when we compare it to the major scale. We'd find that the 3rd note is flattened with respect to the 3rd note of the major scale. Remember, there is a 2tone interval from the 1st to the 3rd note of the major scale.

From this we can make the following **list of triads** and their intervals:

Major :	1	2T	3	$1^1/_2$T	5
Minor :	1	$1^1/_2$T	b3	2T	5
Diminished :	1	$1^1/_2$T	b3	$1^1/_2$T	b5

27.4: **Intervals:** this is the distance from one note to another.

basic intervals :	symbol	distance between notes
semitone :	S	also known as a 'half tone', the smallest interval from one fret to the following fret.
tone :	T	this is a 2 fret distance, for example, from fret 2 to fret 4. It's equal to 2 x Semitones.
minor 3rd :	$1^1/_2$T	the distance of 3 frets we refer to as 'minor 3rd', for example from fret 2 to fret 5.
major 3rd :	2T	a 4 fret distance, or 2 tone interval is a 'major 3rd', for example from fret 2 to fret 6.

28: Chords in each key.

Each key hosts several chords that are built using the notes in these keys. We then use these chords creatively to accompany our melodies in our songs.

Simply select a key, the grid chart will then align the chords that could work best in your selected key.

Please note we have 3 options to build chords from. The major scale, the Melodic minor and the Harmonic minor scale all offer a few different chords. Chords featured are basic chords, there are many more chords we can use!

In section 28. We need to know that the first 6 chords are built from both the major scale and the relative natural minor scale. The following 2 chords are built from the Melodic minor, and the last 2 chords in each row are built from the Harmonic minor scale.

On the left – the major key.   Melodic minor   Harmonic minor

C	Dm	Em	F	G	Am	Bm	D	E	Fm
Db	Ebm	Fm	Gb	Ab	Bbm	Cm	Eb	F	Gbm
D	Em	F#m	G	A	Bm	C#m	E	F#	Gm
Eb	Fm	Gm	Ab	Bb	Cm	Dm	F	G	Abm
E	F#m	G#m	A	B	C#m	D#m	F#	G#	Am
F	Gm	Am	Bb	C	Dm	Em	G	A	Bbm
F#	G#m	A#m	B	C#	D#m	Fm	G#	A#	Bm
G	Am	Bm	C	D	Em	F#	A	B	Cm
Ab	Bbm	Cm	Db	Eb	Fm	G	Bb	C	Dbm
A	Bm	C#m	D	E	F#m	G#	B	C#	Dm
Bb	Cm	Dm	Eb	F	Gm	Am	C	D	Ebm
B	C#m	D#m	E	F#	G#m	A#m	C#	D#	Em

28.1: If you're **composing your own song**, this chart can serve as a guide to which chords often work well together. The sequence of the chords can also determine if you like the chords you've chosen. There are also many other chords we can use, such as suspended, 7th, diminshed, augmented, etc... But, this chart still provides a great starting place!

28.2: Let's say you busy working out a song from your favourite artist and you've worked out most the chords, but one or two are still eluding you. Find the key that has the combination of the chords you already have, and then try some of the other chords that are in the row. There's a good chance the "missing" chord, or chords could be found there. Also bear in mind that some keys have the same chords!

29: Blank guitar neck sheet – useful to photocopy

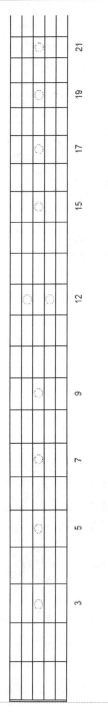  

30: The circle of 5ths:

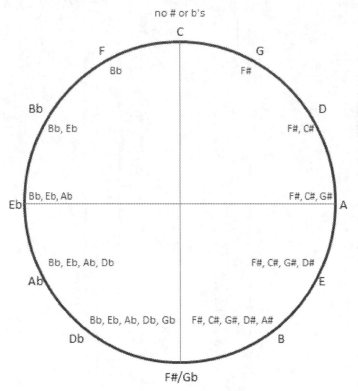

key of:	the # or b notes..
C / Am	no # or B
G / Em	F#
D / Bm	F#, C#
A / F#m	F#, C#, G#
E / C#m	F#, C#, G#, D#
B / G#m	F#, C#, G#, D#, A#
F# / D#m	F#, C#, G#, D#, A#, E#
Gb / Ebm	Bb, Eb, Ab, Db, Gb, Cb
Db / Bbm	Bb, Eb, Ab, Db, Gb
Ab / Fm	Bb, Eb, Ab, Db
Eb / Cm	Bb, Eb, Ab
Bb / Gm	Bb, Eb
F /Dm	Bb
C / Am	no # or B

Please note:

30.1: We need to realize that as we go clockwise, for example from C to G, we get an extra #.

30.2: Similarly, if we go counter-clockwise, from C to F for example, we have an extra b note.

30.3: If we go clockwise, the next key actually starts on the 5th note of the key we were on. For example, the 5th note in the Cmajor scale is G. And the 5th note in the G major scale is D.

30.4: And if we go counter clockwise, the note F is the 5th note of the Cmajor scale when we descend it! Similarly the 5th note of the descending Fmajor scale is Bb.

30.5: Here we can see the **5th note of each major key** being the starting note of the following keys

If we **ascend**, ie: go clockwise

If we **descend**, ie: go anti-clockwise

C	= C D E F G A B C
G	= G A B C D E F# G
D	= D E F# G A B C# D
A	= A B C# D E F# G# A
E	= E F# G# A B C# D# E
B	= B C# D# E F# G# A# B
F#	= F# G# A# B C# D# E F#
Gb	= Gb Ab Bb Cb Db Eb F Gb
Db	= Db Eb F Gb Ab Bb C Db
Ab	= Ab Bb C Db Eb F G Ab
Eb	= Eb F G Ab Bb C D Eb
Bb	= Bb C D Eb F G A Bb
F	= F G A Bb C D E F
C	= C D E F G A B C

C	= C B A G F E D C
F	= F E D C Bb A G F
Bb	= Bb A G F Eb D C Bb
Eb	= Eb D C Bb Ab G F Eb
Ab	= Ab G F Eb Db C Bb Ab
Db	= Db C Bb Ab Gb F Eb Db
Gb	= Gb F Eb Db Cb Bb Ab Gb
F#	= F# E# D# C# B A# G# F#
B	= B A# G# F# E D# C# B
E	= E D# C# B A G# F# E
A	= A G# F# E D C# B A
D	= D C# B A G F# E D
G	= G F# E D C B A G
C	= C B A G F E D C

Ascending (far left)

When going clockwise, we'll observe and extra sharp (#). Until we reach F#, then we have equal flats (♭), and reduce by one flat per key.

Descending (middle left)

Anti-clockwise, we'll observe and extra flat (b). When we reach Gb, we'll have equal sharps (#), and reduce one sharp per key.

Notice that F# and Gb have the same amount of #'s and b's.

30.6: Some interesting facts:

If we compare the Cmajor scale to the 2 closest keys, which are F & G as these two keys have each only one note different from the key of Cmaj, we'd note the following:

Cmajor scale: C D E F G A B C

Fmajor scale : F G A Bb C D E F

Gmajor scale : G A B C D E F# G

We've highlighted the notes that separate these 3 keys from each other, the notes being : F & F#, and B & Bb. Let's now build a scale that has none of these notes, it would look something like this:

Our new scale has these notes : **C D E G A C**

This scale would allow the chords to modulate (change key) using the circle of 5ths, while we could improvise freely not having to worry about notes not common to the reference key. (the reference key in this example being Cmajor) The question now is: "is this scale acceptable?" Yes, we call it the **Pentatonic scale**!

31: Basic Pentatonic theory:

31.1: Penta means 5, and 'tonic' means the root note, the note with the same note name as the note it starts on. (It's also the octave) So 'pentatonic' means it's a 5 note scale, 5 notes per octave! So even though the scale might have 12 notes or more, there are only 5 notes per octave! For example, the Aminor pentatonic scale has the notes: A   C   D   E   G   A

31.2: This scale is possibly the most commonly used scale by rock & blues guitarists. It's ease of use to improvise makes it a favorite for improvising. Please refer to the exercise section of this book to learn some great riffs using it.

31.3: Now, let's look at the keys of Cmaj, Fmaj and Gmajor, as shown below:

Cmajor:	C	D	E	F	G	A	B	C	*Now we'll start*	Cmajor:	C	D	E	F	G	A	B	C
Fmajor:	F	G	A	Bb	C	D	E	F	*the scales on the*	Fmajor:	C	D	E	F	G	A	Bb	C
Gmajor:	G	A	B	C	D	E	F#	G	*same notes ->*	Gmajor:	C	D	E	F#	G	A	Bb	C

31.4: Using Cmajor scale as the reference we notice the only difference between C and Fmajor are the notes Bb & B, similarly the difference between C and G major are F & F#. Now we build a scale using the notes common to all 3 scales. These notes are C D E G A C. Notice, no B or Bb's, or F and F#

31.5: These 5 notes make up the Cmajor Pentatonic scale, which in effect is the same as the Aminor Pentatonic. Now there are 5 positions for the pentatonic scales, one scale for each note within the scale. And, there are also 2 ways to view the five positions. Let's start with the Aminor pentatonic.

> position 1 : The A minor pentatonic - it can be viewed as the pentatonic version of the Aeolian mode
> position 2 : Notes are : C D E G A C, it can be viewed as the pentatonic version of the Ionian mode.
> position 3 : Notes are : D E G A C D, it can be viewed as the pentatonic version of the Dorian mode.
> position 4 : Notes are : E G A C D E, it can be viewed as the pentatonic version of the Phrygian mode.
> position 5 : Notes are : G A C D E G, to be viewed as the pentatonic version of the Mixolydian mode.

31.5: We could also start with the Cmajor pentatonic, and then have 5 positions too. But the norm is to rather work with the minor pentatonic and it's positions. We need to bear in mind that the major pentatonic can be compared to the Ionian mode, which is the major scale too.

> position 1 : Notes are : C D E G A C, this is the major pentatonic scale.
> position 2 : Notes are : D E G A C D, it can be viewed as the pentatonic version of the Dorian mode.
> position 3 : Notes are : E G A C D E, it can be viewed as the pentatonic version of the Phrygian mode.
> position 4 : Notes are : G A C D E G, to be viewed as the pentatonic version of the Mixolydian mode.
> position 5 : Notes are : A C D E G A, to be viewed as the pentatonic version of the Aeolian mode.

32: The Pentatonic scales:

Below are the 5 positions of the Minor Pentatonic scale. Each position simply starts on the 2nd note of the scale shape above it.

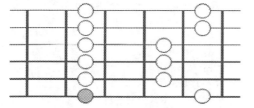

5	Cmaj/Amin
6	**C#maj/A#min**
7	Dmaj/Bmin
8	**Ebmaj/Cmin**
9	Emaj/C#min
10	**Fmaj/Dmin**
11	F#maj/D#min
12	**Gmaj/Emin**
13	Abmaj/Fmin
2	**Amaj/F#mai**
3	Bbmaj/Gmin
4	**Bmaj/G#min**

Position 1: More commonly known as the minor pentatonic scale. (Which can be seen as the equivalent of the natural minor scale.)

Please keep in mind the fret number to the left reflects the key you wish to solo/improvise in.

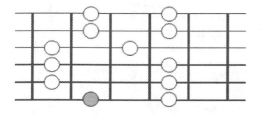

8	Cmaj/Amin
9	**C#maj/A#min**
10	Dmaj/Bmin
11	**Ebmaj/Cmin**
12	Emaj/C#min
13	**Fmaj/Dmin**
2	F#maj/D#min
3	**Gmaj/Emin**
4	Abmaj/Fmin
5	**Amaj/F#mai**
6	Bbmaj/Gmin
7	**Bmaj/G#min**

Position 2: This position can also be seen as the pentatonic equivalent of the Ionian mode. (Which is the same as the major scale.)

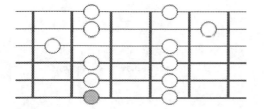

10	Cmaj/Amin
11	**C#maj/A#min**
12	Dmaj/Bmin
13	**Ebmaj/Cmin**
2	Emaj/C#min
3	**Fmaj/Dmin**
4	F#maj/D#min
5	**Gmaj/Emin**
6	Abmaj/Fmin
7	**Amaj/F#mai**
8	Bbmaj/Gmin
9	**Bmaj/G#min**

Position 3: It can also be seen as the pentatonic equivalent of the Dorian mode. (Which is the 2nd mode)

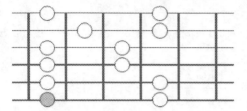

12	Cmaj/Amin
13	**C#maj/A#min**
2	Dmaj/Bmin
3	**Ebmaj/Cmin**
4	Emaj/C#min
5	**Fmaj/Dmin**
6	F#maj/D#min
7	**Gmaj/Emin**
8	Abmaj/Fmin
9	**Amaj/F#mai**
10	Bbmaj/Gmin
11	**Bmaj/G#min**

Position 4: It can also be seen as the pentatonic equivalent of the Phrygian mode. (Which is the 3rd mode)

3	Cmaj/Amin
4	**C#maj/A#min**
5	Dmaj/Bmin
6	**Ebmaj/Cmin**
7	Emaj/C#min
8	**Fmaj/Dmin**
9	F#maj/D#min
10	**Gmaj/Emin**
11	Abmaj/Fmin
12	**Amaj/F#mai**
1	Bbmaj/Gmin
2	**Bmaj/G#m**

Position 5: It can also be seen as the pentatonic equivalent of the Mixolydian mode. (Which is the 5th mode)

Please note: There are no pentatonic equivalent shapes for the Lydian or Locrian shape, as there are 7 modes, but only 5 pentatonic scales.

Reading the Pentatonic scale charts.

1: The highlighted note is the starting note, the scale needs to begin on the fret number on the left!

2: The grid chart allows us to line up the key you need to the starting fret required to play the scale you've selected in the same key.

3: For example, if you're playing the 4th position in the key of Fmaj, we need to start it from the 5th fret. So even though the starting note here would be A, not F, the combined notes in the completed scale are the same as those in the key of Fmajor.

4: All the scales in each key will be the same, provided the starting fret for each scale lines up horizontally with the fret number to the left of it. For example, the key of Em will have the following: Position 1 = fret 12, Position 2 = fret 3, Position 3 = fret 5, Position 4 = fret 7 & Position 5 = fret 10.

33: Basic mode theory:

We get seven modes, one mode for every note in the major scale. The 8th note, the octave, is the same note as the 1st note. The modes names in sequence are: 1) Ionian   2) Dorian   3) Phrygian   4) Lydian   5) Mixolydian   6) Aeolian and 7) Locrian.

33.1: To understand the modes, we need to first see them all in the key of C. We choose Cmaj as it has no #'s or b's.

```
Ionian :   C  T  D  T  E  S  F  T  G  T  A  T  B  S  C
Dorian :   D  T  E  S  F  T  G  T  A  T  B  S  C  T  D
Phrygian : E  S  F  T  G  T  A  T  B  S  C  T  D  T  E
Lydian :   F  T  G  T  A  T  B  S  C  T  D  T  E  S  F
Mixolydian : G  T  A  T  B  S  C  T  D  T  E  S  F  T  G
Aeolian :  A  T  B  S  C  T  D  T  E  S  F  T  G  T  A
locrian :  B  S  C  T  D  T  E  S  F  T  G  T  A  T  B
```

Please observe that although all modes contain the same notes, they each have different intervals. 'ie: the T T S.. Sequence changes with each mode. The next step is to start each mode on the same note and observe the differences in each mode.

33.2: Here we have all the modes starting on the same note, once more C. Please bear in mind that only the Ionian mode is the major scale, this is why the notes are the same.

```
           1     2     3     4     5     6     7     8
Ionian :   C  T  D  T  E  S  F  T  G  T  A  T  B  S  C
Dorian :   C  T  D  S  Eb T  F  T  G  T  A  S  Bb T  C
Phrygian : C  S  Db T  Eb T  F  T  G  S  Ab T  Bb T  C
Lydian :   C  T  D  T  E  T  F# S  G  T  A  T  B  S  C
Mixolydian : C  T  D  T  E  S  F  T  G  T  A  S  Bb T  C
Aeolian :  C  T  D  S  Eb T  F  T  G  S  Ab T  Bb T  C
locrian :  C  S  Db T  Eb T  F  S  Gb T  Ab T  Bb T  C
```

Now we find we have a few sharps & flats in the modes. We've added position numbers at the top. This way we compare the changes in each mode, using the Ionian as the reference. For example, the Lydian has a #4th note when compared to the Ionian.

33.3: Comparing all the modes to the Ionian mode we'd end up with the following list of characteristics. Bear in mind the Ionian is the major scale, and the major scale serves as the reference to all music theory.

Ionian : reference
Dorian : b3 & b7
Phrygian : b2, b3, b6 & b7
Lydian : #4
Mixolydian : b7
Aeolian : b3, b6 & b7
locrian : b2, b3, b5, b6 & b7

Now, if we refer to the chapter on chord construction, we'd understand the characteristics of the chords as listed here. This is just the beginning of comparing the modes to the chords.

```
major :      1   3   5
minor :      1   b3  5
diminished : 1   b3  b5
```

```
major7 :  1   3   5   7
min7 :    1   b3  5   b7
7 :       1   3   5   b7
m7b5 :    1   b3  b5  b7
```

33.4: <u>Let's compare the modes</u> to the chords in greater detail:

The **Dorian mode** has **b3 & b7** notes. Now the minor & min7 chords also have these characteristics. So we could improvise a C Dorian mode over a **Cmin** or **Cmin7** chord. We also say that the Dorian is minor related. Minor related means we can build a minor chord from it's root position.

The **Phrygian** also works with the **min** and **min7**. Even though the Phrygian has a b2 & b6 too, the chords used here don't use these notes. We'll discuss this later with 'bigger chords like 9th, 11th & 13th's.

The **Lydian** mode is major related as the only altered note is the **#4**, which has no conflicts with the notes found in the major or maj7 chords.

The **Mixolydian** mode has a **b7**, which is works well with the major chord, but the maj7 cannot work here, this time we need the **'dominant7'**, written simply as **'7'**. This mode is also major related.

Mode 6, the **Aeolian**, is the also known as the **natural minor** scale. This mode also compliments the **min** and **min7** chords. The b6 note has no effect on these 2 chords as the chords do not have a 6th note present.

Lastly, the **Locrian** has the most altered notes. This mode works for the **diminished & m7b5** chord. The mode is neither major nor minor related due to the **b5**. But, it is closer to the minor than the major due to b3rd.

33.5: <u>Basic summary so far...</u>

33.5..1: We have 7 modes, each mode has 7 notes. We refer to any 7 notes scale or mode as 'diatonic'.

33.5.2: If the modes contain the same notes, we refer to them as 'related'. For example the D Dorian mode is related to the Cmajor scale. Similarly the B Aeolian is related to the D Ionian. Use the grid method on the following page to check this.

33.5.3 : The Ionian mode is the major scale and the Aeolian mode is the natural minor scale.

33.5.4 : Each major key has a relative minor. The relative minor of each major scale will be found 3 frets (a minor 3rd interval) down. For example the relative minor of C major is A minor. Remember that they're related as both have the same notes!

34: The Modes – block positions:

Below are the 7 positions of the Modes. Each position simply starts on the 2nd note of the scale shape above it.

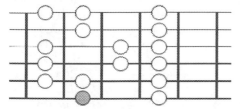

34.1: The Ionian mode is position 1. All the other modes are compared to this mode. It is also known as the major scale.

intervals : T T S T T T S

8	Cmaj/Amin	C Ionian
9	C#maj/A#min	C# Ionian
10	Dmaj/Bmin	D Ionian
11	Ebmaj/Cmin	Eb Ionian
12	Emaj/C#min	E Ionian
13	Fmaj/Dmin	F Ionian
2	F#maj/D#min	F# Ionian
3	Gmaj/Emin	G Ionian
4	Abmaj/Fmin	Ab Ionian
5	Amaj/F#mai	A Ionian
6	Bbmaj/Gmin	Bb Ionian
7	Bmai/G#min	B Ionian

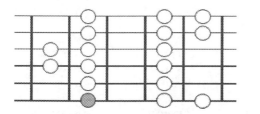

34.2: The 2nd position, the **Dorian** has a b3 and b7 w.r.t. the Ionian, it minor related due to the b3.

intervals : T S T T T S T

10	Cmaj/Amin	D Dorian
11	C#maj/A#min	D# Dorian
12	Dmaj/Bmin	E Dorian
13	Ebmaj/Cmin	F Dorian
2	Emaj/C#min	F# Dorian
3	Fmaj/Dmin	G Dorian
4	F#maj/D#min	G# Dorian
5	Gmaj/Emin	A Dorian
6	Abmaj/Fmin	Bb Dorian
7	Amaj/F#mai	B Dorian
8	Bbmaj/Gmin	C Dorian
9	Bmaj/G#min	C# Dorian

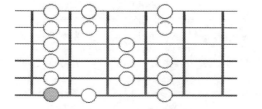

34.3 The 3rd position, **the Phrygian**, has a b2, b3, b6 & b7 w.r.t. the Ionian. It is also minor related, and the b2 can be viewed as a b9.

intervals : S T T T S T T

12	Cmaj/Amin	E Phrygian
1	C#maj/A#min	F Phrygian
2	Dmaj/Bmin	F# Phrygian
3	Ebmaj/Cmin	G Phrygian
4	Emaj/C#min	G# Phrygian
5	Fmaj/Dmin	A Phrygian
6	F#maj/D#min	A# Phrygian
7	Gmaj/Emin	B Phrygian
8	Abmaj/Fmin	C Phrygian
9	Amaj/F#mai	C# Phrygian
10	Bbmaj/Gmin	D Phrygian
11	Bmaj/G#min	D# Phrygian

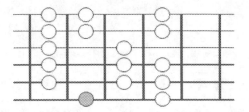

13	Cmaj/Amin	F Lydian
2	**C#maj/A#min**	**F# Lydian**
3	Dmaj/Bmin	G Lydian
4	**Ebmaj/Cmin**	**Ab Lydian**
5	Emaj/C#min	A Lydian
6	**Fmaj/Dmin**	**Bb Lydian**
7	F#maj/D#min	B Lydian
8	**Gmaj/Emin**	**C Lydian**
9	Abmaj/Fmin	Db Lydian
10	**Amaj/F#mai**	**D Lydian**
11	Bbmaj/Gmin	Eb Lydian
12	**Bmaj/G#min**	**E Lydian**

34.4: The **Lydian mode** at 4th position, is similar to the Ionian, but for the #4, which can also be viewed as a #11. It is major related..

intervals : T T S T T S

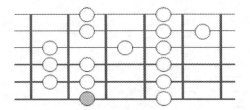

3	Cmaj/Amin	G Mixolydian
4	**C#maj/A#min**	**G# Mixolydian**
5	Dmaj/Bmin	A Mixolydian
6	**Ebmaj/Cmin**	**Bb Mixolydian**
7	Emaj/C#min	B Mixolydian
8	**Fmaj/Dmin**	**C Mixolydian**
9	F#maj/D#min	C# Mixolydian
10	**Gmaj/Emin**	**D Mixolydian**
11	Abmaj/Fmin	Eb Mixolydian
12	**Amaj/F#mai**	**E Mixolydian**
13	Bbmaj/Gmin	F Mixolydian
2	**Bmaj/G#min**	**F# Mixolydian**

34.5: Position 5 of the major scale allows us to build the **Mixolydian mode,** which is also major related. It has a b7, also referred to as a dominant 7.

intervals : T T S T T S T

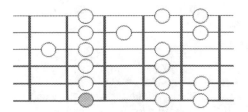

5	Cmaj/Amin	A Aeoilian
6	**C#maj/A#min**	**A# Aeolian**
7	Dmaj/Bmin	B Aeolian
8	**Ebmaj/Cmin**	**C Aeolian**
9	Emaj/C#min	C# Aeolian
10	**Fmaj/Dmin**	**D Aeolian**
11	F#maj/D#min	D# Aeolian
12	**Gmaj/Emin**	**E Aeolian**
13	Abmaj/Fmin	F Aeolian
2	**Amaj/F#mai**	**F# Aeolian**
3	Bbmaj/Gmin	G Aeolian
4	**Bmaj/G#min**	**G# Aeolian**

34.6: The **Aeolian mode** at position 6 is also known as the natural minor scale. It has a b3, b6 and b7 w.r.t. the major scale.

intervals : T S T T S T T

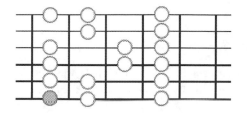

7	Cmaj/Amin	B Locrian
8	C#maj/A#min	B# Locrian
9	Dmaj/Bmin	C# Locrian
10	Ebmaj/Cmin	D Locrian
11	Emaj/C#min	D# Locrian
12	Fmaj/Dmin	E Locrian
13	F#maj/D#min	E# Locrian
2	Gmaj/Emin	F# Locrian
3	Abmaj/Fmin	G Locrian
4	Amaj/F#mai	G# Locrian
5	Bbmaj/Gmin	A Locrian
6	Bmaj/G#min	A# Locrian

34.7: The 7th mode, **the Locrian**, provides us a diminished due to the b5. It's 2, 3, 5, 6 & 7th notes are all flat w.r.t. the Ionian.

intervals : S T T S T T T

Reading the Mode scale charts.

1: The highlighted note is the starting note, the scale needs to begin on the fret number on the left!

2: The grid chart allows us to line up the key you need to the starting fret required to play the scale you've selected in the same key.

3: For example, if you're playing the Dorian mode in the key of Emaj, we need to start it from the 2nd fret. So even though the starting note here would be G#, not E, the combined notes in the completed scale are the same as those in the key of Emajor.

4: All the scales in each key will be the same, provided the starting fret for each scale lines up horizontally with the fret number to the left of it. For example, the key of E will have the following: Ionian = fret 12, Dorian = fret 2, Phrygian = fret 4, Lydian 4 = fret 5, Mixolydian = fret 7, Aeolian = fret 9 & the Locrian = fret 11.

35: Basic Minor Blues theory:

The minor blues scale is basically the minor pentatonic scale with a flattened 5th tone added. (b5)

35.1: To demonstrate this, we're going to list the notes of the Aminor Pentatonic scale, then show the Amajor scale from where we'll take the 5th note and flatten it. Lastly we'll combine the b5 note with the minor pentatonic and end up with our Minor Blues scale.

35.1.1: The notes in the **Aminor Pentatonic** scale are : **A C D E G A**

35.1 2: The notes in the **Amajor** scale are : **A B C# D E F# G# A**

35.1.3: The **5th** note of the A major scale is **E**, if we **flatten** this, we have **Eb**.

35.1. 4: We **add the Eb** to the minor pentatonic scale = the **Aminor blues: A C D Eb E G A**

We refer to the **b5** as the **'blues note'** of this scale. As a general rule, when improvising we use the blues note as a **passing note**, which add tonal variety, but stopping on the 5bth note can often sound dissonant. When we look at a basic blues progression, for example a 12 bar blues in A, we'll find out why!

35.2: A basic 12 bars blues progression would normally go like this:

A7   /A7   /A7   /A7   /D7   /D7   /A7   /A7   /E7   /D7   /A7   /E7

35.3: Next we analyze the notes that are used to build each of the chords, this will give us the target notes. The notes that are found in the chords are referred to as chord tones!

The chord A7 consists of these notes : A   C#   E   G

The chord D7 consists of these notes : D   F#   A   C

The chord E7 consists of these notes : E   G#   B   D

35.3.1: A target note is the note we stop on when we end a riff or phrase. It has to compliment the chord that is being played at the same point in time, this is why we need to know the notes in each chord.

35.4: Here are some ideas for when we're applying the scale when improvising. Please bear in mind that we working with a standard 12 bar progression in A.

35.4.1: We can start any-where in the scale, remember that lingering on any note also often implies a target note, so just be careful! Keep in mind the chord tones!

35.4.2: It's not the amount of notes we play, or how fast we play - this is your creative choice, so play what you think sounds good. There is no absolute as to what notes must be played, but the most important guideline is to stop on a target note. Target notes and chord tones should complement each other.

35.4.3: While the chord A7 is being played, the notes A, E & G from the Aminor blues scale compliment the chords notes. While the notes C, D & Eb are not found in the chord. So we can play them, but we should try not to stop or linger on them!

36.4.4: When D7 is being played, the Aminor blues scale offers the notes A, C & D as target notes. This time Eb, E & G will not make good target notes, but once more, please use them as passing notes.

35.4.5: Lastly, the notes D & E from the Aminor blues scale compliment the E7 chord. Please observe that the Eb, called the minor blue note, doesn't find a chord tone in any of the chords, but it makes a great passing note, giving us that classic Blues sound!

36: The Minor Blues scales

Even though the Minor Blues scale is a favorite with Blues and Jazz players, we can use any scale for any style of music! There are no absolutes.

Certain scales are arguably more popular in certain styles of music, but I'd recommend that a good player has a good knowledge of as many scales as possible. This in turn will allow them a wide tonal variety to express themselves with.

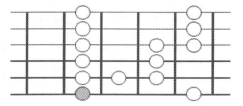

5	Cmaj/Amin
6	**C#maj/A#min**
7	Dmaj/Bmin
8	**Ebmaj/Cmin**
9	Emaj/C#min
10	**Fmaj/Dmin**
11	F#maj/D#min
12	**Gmaj/Emin**
13	Abmaj/Fmin
2	**Amaj/F#mai**
3	Bbmaj/Gmin
4	**Bmaj/G#min**

Position 1: This shape is similar to the minor Pentatonic scales 1st position. Please observe the 3 chromatic notes.

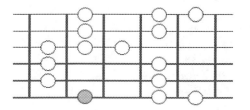

8	Cmaj/Amin
9	**C#maj/A#min**
10	Dmaj/Bmin
11	**Ebmaj/Cmin**
12	Emaj/C#min
13	**Fmaj/Dmin**
2	F#maj/D#min
3	**Gmaj/Emin**
4	Abmaj/Fmin
5	**Amaj/F#mai**
6	Bbmaj/Gmin
7	**Bmaj/G#min**

Position 2: This position is very similar to the Major shape. All the positions listed here will have exactly the same notes, simply starting from a different position within the scale.

Reading the Minor Blues scale charts.

1: The highlighted note is the starting note, the scale needs to begin on the fret number on the left!

2: Use the grid chart to line up the key required to the starting fret of the play the selected scale.

3: For example, if playing the 4th position in the key of Fmaj, play it from fret 5th. Even though the starting note is A, not F, the combined notes are as needed for the key of Fmajor.

4: All the scales in each key will be the same, provided the starting fret for each scale lines up horizontally with the fret number to the left of it. For example, the key of Em will have the following: Position 1 = fret 12, Position 2 = fret 3, Position 3 = fret 5, Position 4 = fret 7 & Position 5 = fret 10.

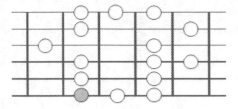

10	Cmaj/Amin
11	**C#maj/A#min**
12	Dmaj/Bmin
13	**Ebmaj/Cmin**
2	Emaj/C#min
3	**Fmaj/Dmin**
4	F#maj/D#min
5	**Gmaj/Emin**
6	Abmaj/Fmin
7	**Amaj/F#mai**
8	Bbmaj/Gmin
9	**Bmaj/G#min**

Position 3: This position begins with the chromatic run. Please observe that although this scale may start on D, it is still in the key of Cmaj and Aminor.

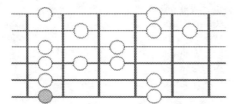

12	Cmaj/Amin
13	**C#maj/A#min**
2	Dmaj/Bmin
3	**Ebmaj/Cmin**
4	Emaj/C#min
5	**Fmaj/Dmin**
6	F#maj/D#min
7	**Gmaj/Emin**
8	Abmaj/Fmin
9	**Amaj/F#mai**
10	Bbmaj/Gmin
11	**Bmaj/G#min**

Position 4: The fingering of this shape might be more challenging at lower frets due to the frets being wider. But once more, all the notes are the same, provided the key you've selected is the same. For example, in Emajor, this scale must be played from fret 4!

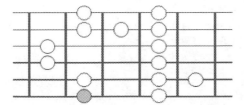

3	Cmaj/Amin
4	**C#maj/A#min**
5	Dmaj/Bmin
6	**Ebmaj/Cmin**
7	Emaj/C#min
8	**Fmaj/Dmin**
9	F#maj/D#min
10	**Gmaj/Emin**
11	Abmaj/Fmin
12	**Amaj/F#mai**
13	Bbmaj/Gmin
2	**Bmaj/G#min**

Position 5: The last of the 5 positions. If we want to work up the fret board from this scale, we'll work ourselves back into position1..

37: Basic Major Blues scale theory

The major blues scale can be compared to the minor pentatonic scale with the 3rd note of the major scale added. This scale's unique for having the major and minor 3rd present at the same time!

37.1: To demonstrate this, we're going to list the notes of the Aminor Pentatonic scale, then show the Amajor scale from where we'll take the 3rd note. Then we'll combine the 3rd note with the minor pentatonic and end up with our Major Blues scale.

37.1.1: The notes in the Aminor Pentatonic scale are : **A C D E G A**

37.1.2: The notes in the Amajor scale are : **A B C# D E F# G# A**

37.1.3: The 3rd note of the A major scale is **C#.**

37.1.4: We add the C# to the minor pentatonic scale = the Amajor blues: **A C C# D E G A**

We refer to the 3rd as the 'blues note' of this scale. Unlike the minor blues note, the maj3rd note can be used as a target note, depending on which chord is being played at the time of us wanting to resolve on it. When we look at a basic blues progression, for example a 12 bar blues in A, we'll find out why!

37.2: A basic 12 bars blues progression would normally go like this :

A7   /A7   /A7   /A7   /D7   /D7   /A7   /A7   /E7   /D7   /A7   /E7

37.3: Next we analyze the notes that are used to build each of the chords, this will give us the target notes. The notes that are found in the chords are referred to as chord tones!

The chord A7 consists of these notes : A   C#   E   G

The chord D7 consists of these notes : D   F#   A   C

The chord E7 consists of these notes : E   G#   B   D

37.3.1: A target note is the note we stop on when we end a riff or phrase. It has to compliment the chord that is being played at the same point in time, this is why we need to know the notes in each chord.

37.4: Here are some ideas for when we're applying the scale when improvising. (Please bear mind that we working with a standard 12 bar progression in A)

37.4.1: We can start any-where in the scale, remember that lingering on any note also often implies a target note, so just be careful! Keep in mind the chord tones!

37.4.2: It's not about the amount of notes we play, or how fast we play them - this is your creative choice, so play what you think sounds good. There is no absolute as to what notes must be played, but the most important guideline is to stop on a target note. Target notes and chord tones should compliment each other.

37.4.3: While the chord **A7** is being played, the notes **A, C#, E & G** from the Amajor blues scale compliment the chords notes. While the notes **C & D** are not found in the chord. So we can play them, but we should try not to stop or linger on them!

37.4.4: When **D7** is being played, the Amajor blues scale offers the notes **A, C & D** as target notes. This time **C#, E & G** will not make good target notes, but once more, please use them as passing notes.

37.4.5: Lastly, the notes **D & E** from the Amajor blues scale compliment the **E7** chord.

38: The Major Blues scales:

As with the Minor Blues scale, the Major blues scales are equally useful for any style of music. From rock to reggae, from blues to jazz. We can use any scale for any style of music! There are no absolutes.

Certain scales are arguably more popular in certain styles of music, but I'd recommend that a good player has a good knowledge of as many scales as possible. This in turn will allow them a wide tonal variety to express themselves with.

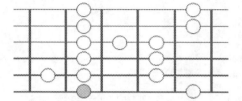

5	Cmaj/Amin
6	**C#maj/A#min**
7	Dmaj/Bmin
8	**Ebmaj/Cmin**
9	Emaj/C#min
10	**Fmaj/Dmin**
11	F#maj/D#min
12	**Gmaj/Emin**
13	Abmaj/Fmin
2	**Amaj/F#mai**
3	Bbmaj/Gmin
4	**Bmaj/G#min**

Position 1: This shape is similar to the minor Pentatonic scales 1st position. Please observe the 3 chromatic notes.

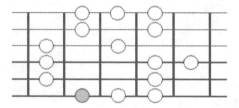

8	Cmaj/Amin
9	**C#maj/A#min**
10	Dmaj/Bmin
11	**Ebmaj/Cmin**
12	Emaj/C#min
13	**Fmaj/Dmin**
2	F#maj/D#min
3	**Gmaj/Emin**
4	Abmaj/Fmin
5	**Amaj/F#mai**
6	Bbmaj/Gmin
7	**Bmaj/G#min**

Position 2: This position is very similar to the Major pentatonic shape. All the positions listed here will have exactly the same notes, simply starting from a different position within the scale.

Reading the Major Blues scale charts.

1: The highlighted note is the starting note, the scale needs to begin on the fret number on the leftt!

2: Use the grid chart to line up the key required to the starting fret of the play the selected scale.

3: For example, if playing the 4th position in the key of Fmaj, play it from fret 5th. Even though the starting note is A, not F, the combined notes are as needed for the key of Fmajor.

4: All the scales in each key will be the same, provided the starting fret for each scale lines up horizontally with the fret number to the left of it. For example, the key of Em will have the following: Position 1 = fret 12, Position 2 = fret 3, Position 3 = fret 5, Position 4 = fret 7 & Position 5 = fret 10.

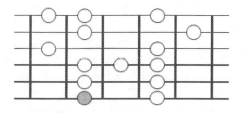

10	Cmaj/Amin
11	**C#maj/A#min**
12	Dmaj/Bmin
13	**Ebmaj/Cmin**
2	Emaj/C#min
3	**Fmaj/Dmin**
4	F#maj/D#min
5	**Gmaj/Emin**
6	Abmaj/Fmin
7	**Amaj/F#mai**
8	Bbmaj/Gmin
9	**Bmaj/G#min**

Position 3: This position begins with the chromatic run. Please observe that although this scale may start on D, it is still in the key of Cmaj and Aminor.

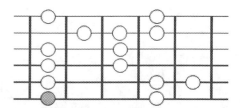

12	Cmaj/Amin
13	**C#maj/A#min**
2	Dmaj/Bmin
3	**Ebmaj/Cmin**
4	Emaj/C#min
5	**Fmaj/Dmin**
6	F#maj/D#min
7	**Gmaj/Emin**
8	Abmaj/Fmin
9	**Amaj/F#mai**
10	Bbmaj/Gmin
11	**Bmaj/G#min**

Position 4: The fingering of this shape might be more challenging at lower frets due to the frets being wider. But once more, all the notes are the same, provided the key you've selected is the same. For example, in Emajor, this scale must be played from fret 4!

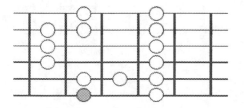

3	Cmaj/Amin
4	**C#maj/A#min**
5	Dmaj/Bmin
6	**Ebmaj/Cmin**
7	Emaj/C#min
8	**Fmaj/Dmin**
9	F#maj/D#min
10	**Gmaj/Emin**
11	Abmaj/Fmin
12	**Amaj/F#mai**
13	Bbmaj/Gmin
2	**Bmaj/G#min**

Position 5: The last of the 5 positions. If we want to work up the fret board from this scale, we'll work ourselves back into position1..

39: Scale options within a key:

We have several type of scales, such as the pentatonic, the modes, major & minor blues scales, harmonic minor and also the melodic minor. There is NO law that say we may not combine them! Although there are some guidelines on how to do this successfully. The key word here is target notes and chord tones.

Let's assume the key of Aminor, which is the relative minor of Cmajor. Neither of these have any #'s or b's. When we compare the other scales we can now see the 'accidentals', or the notes that separate the other scale types from the natural minor scale. (Remember the natural minor is also known as the Aeolian, which is in turn built from the 6th note of the Cmajor scale - known as the C Ionian mode.)

Below we've put the A natural minor scale in the middle, and the other related modes and scales with their characteristic around it. The concept is to compare the differences, and feel free to use ANY of the other scales. We just need to keep in mind the chords that are being played, and that it is best to resolve on one of the notes within the chord being played at that point of time! We call these notes "target notes". In other words, "chord tones" which are the notes that make up the chord are our ideal target notes.

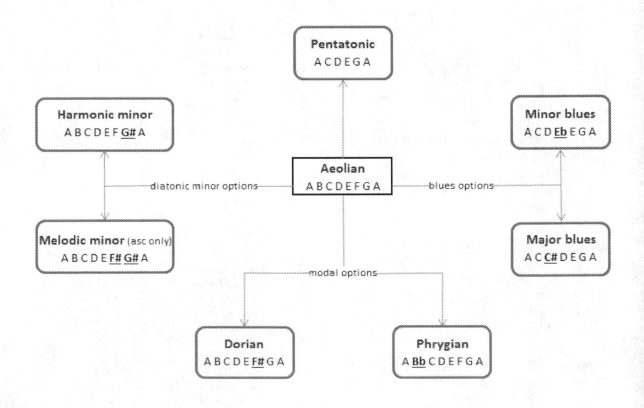

39.1: Please observe the following:

39.1.1: All the above scales can be used to solo within the key of **Aminor** (or **Cmajor**)

39.1.2: The note we resolve, or stop on will determine if the phrase sounds good or not - we need to be aware of the chord structure, and where we are in the chord progression. Ie: the time line!

39.1.3: We can combine any of the scales together too. This will result in some great chromatic phrases! Once more, watch your target notes!!

For example, we can combine the major and minor blues scale, and get to use the notes : **A C C# D Eb E G A**, this give us the chromatic run of **C - C# - D - Eb - E**.

We can even combine the A Dorian & A Phrygian, and get the notes : **A Bb B C D E F F# G A**. Now we have 2 chromatic runs, **A - Bb - B - C**, as well **as E - F - F# - G**.

39.1.4: Nothing is stopping us from combining points 3.2 & 3.3, we'll now combine the modal options with the two blues scales and have these notes : **A - Bb - B - C - C# - D - Eb - E - F - F# - G - A**. this is almost completely chromatic. All we need to do is add the harmonic or melodic minor? Which we can do too!

39.1.5: To summarize, we can combine any of the scales at any time. BUT, it's a good idea to keep in mind the Aeolian mode as a source or foundation. And of course, we cannot stress enough the importance of target notes and chord tones. Let your ear be the guide and experiment. Music is an ART FORM. So if it sounds good, do it! In short, enjoy..

39.1.6: There are some classical laws and theory that will open even more idea's with respect to melody and harmony ideas. The purpose of this book is an overview for chord and scale reference, not pages of theory. Please consult with a good classical music teacher for more detailed explanations.

40: the 3 types of minor scale:

We get 3 types of minor scale: 1) the Natural minor, 2) the Harmonic minor & 3) the Melodic minor scale.

By using our grid system, we can see which notes are common to all 3 scale types, and also the unique characteristic of each scale.

40.1: The natural minor

This scale has the same notes as the relative major. For example, the notes in Cmajor and Aminor are identical. This scale is also refered to as the Aeolian mode, which is built from the 6th note of the major scale.

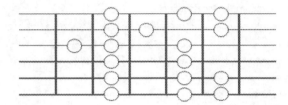

40.2: The Harmonic minor

This scale can be viewed as the natural minor scale with a major 7th. The minor 3rd interval from the F to the G# allows us to have a major, minor and diminished triad being built from the 6th notes position.

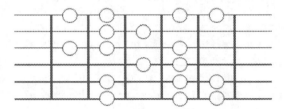

40.3: The Melodic minor

On ascending only, this scale can be compared to the natural minor, with a major 6th and 7th notes. These notes are # with respect to the natural minor. BUT, when descending, it IS the natural minor - see the Melodic minor page.

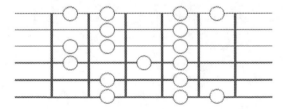

41.2: Harmonic minor theory:

Every major key has a relative minor, in other words a minor scale that contains the same notes as the major key it's related to, but simply starting on a different note. The minor scale starts on the 6th note of the related major scale. We refer to this minor scale as the 'natural' minor. The natural minor's modal name is Aeolian.

Now we'll compare the Cmajor scale to the Aminor. (the A natural minor)

C T D T E S F T G T A T B S C = Cmaj scale
A T B S C T D T E S F T G T A = Amin scale

41.1: Now, we get 3 types of minor scales, let's compare them starting on the note A:

natural minor : A T B S C T D T E S F T G T A
melodic minor : A T B S C T D T E T F# T G# S A
harmonic minor : A T B S C T D T E S F 1½ G# S A

41.2: The **Harmonic minor** scale's **unique characteristic** is the **min3rd** interval between the **6 & 7th** notes. *Please also observe that the harmonic minor ascends and descends with the same notes, unlike the Melodic minor which descends like the natural minor*

A T B S C T D T E S F 1½ G# S A

As with modes, we have 7 positions within the harmonic minor scale, these are:
(Please note that for comparison purposes only, we're going to compare to the A natural minor.)

note positions:	1	2	3	4	5	6	7	8		1	2	3	4	5	6	7	8	note positions:
A Harmonic Minor :	A	B	C	D	E	F	G#	A		A	B	C	D	E	F	G	A	: A Natural Minor
B Locrian #6 :	B	C	D	E	F	G#	A	B		B	C	D	E	F	G	A	B	: B Locrian
C Ionian #5 :	C	D	E	F	G#	A	B	C		C	D	E	F	G	A	B	C	: C Ionian
D Dorian #4 :	D	E	F	G#	A	B	C	D		D	E	F	G	A	B	C	D	: D Dorian
E Phrygian #3 :	E	F	G#	A	B	C	D	E		E	F	G	A	B	C	D	E	: E Phrygian
F Lydian #2 :	F	G#	A	B	C	D	E	F		F	G	A	B	C	D	E	F	: F Lydian
G# Mixolydian #1 :	G#	A	B	C	D	E	F	G#		G	A	B	C	D	E	F	G	: G Mixolydian

41.3: To appreciate the Harmonic minor mode names, let's look at the notes in the B Locrian #6 mode and compare it to the standard B Locrian mode. We'll notice the 6th note is a 'G#' in the Locrian #6, while we have a G in the standard B Locrian mode. Because we compare the Harmonic minor modes to the standard modes, we now see the 6th note of the Locrian #6 is sharpened, and this is how it gets it's name.

The key to understanding how the Harmonic modes get their names, is to compare it to the standard modes. We do this as the standard modes are all derived from positions on the Major scale, and we should know by now that the major scales is our reference.

41.4 Basic triads in the key of A Harmonic minor:

(due to the min 3rd interval, we can now build several triads from some of the positions of this scale.)

chords built with ascending notes :   Am   Bdim   Caug   D   E   F   G#dim

                                        Ddim   Fm   G#aug

                                                                Fdim

Observe the notes within these chords:

chord:		notes..			chord:		notes..			chord:		notes..		
D	=	D	F#	A	F	=	F	A	C	G#dim	=	G#	B	D
Ddim	=	D	F	G#	Fm	=	F	G#	C	G#aug	=	G#	C	E
					Fdim	=	F	G#	B					

(Please observe that all the notes found in the chords listed above can be found in the Aharmonic minor scale)

(Please observe that all the notes found in the chords listed above can be found in the A harmonic minor scale)

42: The Harmonic minor scales:

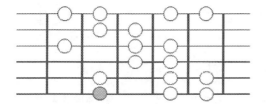

5	Cmaj/Amin	A Harmonic
6	**C#maj/A#min**	**Bb Harmonic**
7	Dmaj/Bmin	B Harmonic
8	**Ebmaj/Cmin**	**C Harmonic**
9	Emaj/C#min	C# Harmonic
10	**Fmaj/Dmin**	**D Harmonic**
11	F#maj/D#min	Eb Harmonic
12	**Gmaj/Emin**	**E Harmonic**
13	Abmaj/Fmin	F Harmonic
2	**Amaj/F#mai**	**F# Harmonic**
3	Bbmaj/Gmin	G Harmonic
4	**Bmaj/G#min**	**G# Harmonic**

42.1: __The Harmonic minor__ is position 1. When comparing to the natural minor, please observe that the 7th note and it's octave is raised (#) for the harmonic minor. At fret 5 this is the A harmonic minor.

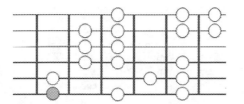

7	Cmaj/Amin	B Locrian #6
8	**C#maj/A#min**	**C Locrian#6**
9	Dmaj/Bmin	C# Locrian#6
10	**Ebmaj/Cmin**	**D Locrian#6**
11	Emaj/C#min	D# Locrian#6
12	**Fmaj/Dmin**	**E Locrian#6**
13	F#maj/D#min	F Locrian#6
2	**Gmaj/Emin**	**F# Locrian#6**
3	Abmaj/Fmin	G Locrian#6
4	**Amaj/F#mai**	**G# Locrian#6**
5	Bbmaj/Gmin	A Locrian#6
6	**Bmaj/G#min**	A# Locrian #6

42.2: Position 2 is the **Locrian #6** mode. Remember to compare these to the normal modes. If we compare this to the Locrian mode, we'll notice the above scales 6th note, and it's octaves are raised, or sharpened. (#)

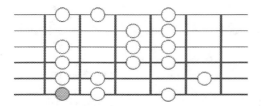

8	Cmaj/Amin	C Ionian #5
9	**C#maj/A#min**	C# Ionian#5
10	Dmaj/Bmin	D Ionian#5
11	**Ebmaj/Cmin**	**Eb Ionian#5**
12	Emaj/C#min	E Ionian#5
13	**Fmaj/Dmin**	**F Ionian#5**
2	F#maj/D#min	F# Ionian#5
3	**Gmaj/Emin**	**G Ionian#5**
4	Abmaj/Fmin	Ab Ionian#5
5	**Amaj/F#mai**	**A Ionian#5**
6	Bbmaj/Gmin	Bb Ionian#5
7	**Bmaj/G#min**	**B Ionian #5**

42.3: Position 3 is the **Ionian #5** mode. Once more, when we compare this to the normal Ionian mode we'll notice the above scales 5th note, and it's octaves are raised, or sharpened. (#)

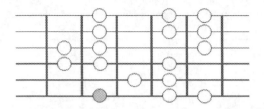

10	Cmaj/Amin	D Dorian #4
11	**C#maj/A#min**	**D# Dorian#4**
12	Dmaj/Bmin	E Dorian#4
13	**Ebmaj/Cmin**	**F Dorian#4**
2	Emaj/C#min	F# Dorian#4
3	**Fmaj/Dmin**	**G Dorian#4**
4	F#maj/D#min	G# Dorian#4
5	**Gmaj/Emin**	**A Dorian#4**
6	Abmaj/Fmin	Bb Dorian#4
7	**Amaj/F#mai**	**B Dorian#4**
8	Bbmaj/Gmin	C Dorian#4
9	**Bmaj/G#min**	**C# Dorian #4**

42.4: **Position 4** is the **Dorian #4** mode. Here we'll observe the only difference between this mode and the Dorian mode is the 4th note that is raised here.

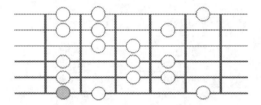

12	Cmaj/Amin	E Phrygian #3
13	**C#maj/A#min**	**F Phrygian#3**
2	Dmaj/Bmin	F# Phrygian#3
3	**Ebmaj/Cmin**	**G Phrygian#3**
4	Emaj/C#min	G# Phrygian#3
5	**Fmaj/Dmin**	**A Phrygian#3**
6	F#maj/D#min	A# Phrygian#3
7	**Gmaj/Emin**	**B Phrygian#3**
8	Abmaj/Fmin	C Phrygian#3
9	**Amaj/F#mai**	**C# Phrygian#3**
10	Bbmaj/Gmin	D Phrygian#3
11	**Bmaj/G#min**	**D# Phrygian#3**

42.5: **Position 5** is the **Phrygian #3** mode. Normally the Phrygian is minor related due to the b3rd. but with raised 3rd, or major 3rd, the Phrygian #3 is actually major related.

13	Cmaj/Amin	F Lydian #2
2	**C#maj/A#min**	**F# Lydian#2**
3	Dmaj/Bmin	G Lydian#2
4	**Ebmaj/Cmin**	**Ab Lydian#2**
5	Emaj/C#min	A Lydian#2
6	**Fmaj/Dmin**	**Bb Lydian#2**
7	F#maj/D#min	B Lydian#2
8	**Gmaj/Emin**	**C Lydian#2**
9	Abmaj/Fmin	Db Lydian#2
10	**Amaj/F#mai**	**D Lydian#2**
11	Bbmaj/Gmin	Eb Lydian#2
12	**Bmaj/G#min**	**E Lydian #2**

42.6: **Position 6** is the **Lydian #2** mode. This mode has both a major & minor 3rd, allowing for either triad. The presence of the #4 (which is the same note as a b5) allows for diminished as a 3rd triad option.

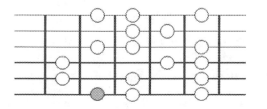

4	Cmaj/Amin	G# Mixolydian #1
5	C#maj/A#min	A Mixolydian#1
6	Dmaj/Bmin	A# Mixolydian#1
7	Ebmaj/Cmin	B Mixolydian#1
8	Emaj/C#min	C Mixolydian#1
9	Fmaj/Dmin	C# Mixolydian#1
10	F#maj/D#min	D Mixolydian#1
11	Gmaj/Emin	D# Mixolydian#1
12	Abmaj/Fmin	E Mixolydian#1
13	Amaj/F#mai	F Mixolydian#1
2	Bbmaj/Gmin	F# Mixolydian#1
3	Bmaj/G#min	G Mixolydian#1

42.7: **Position 7,** our last is the **Mixolydian #1** mode. Here we'll observe the only difference between this mode and the Mixolydian mode is the root note that is raised here.

Reading the Harmonic scale charts.

1: The highlighted note is the starting note, the scale needs to begin on the fret number on the left!

2: The grid chart allows us to line up the key you need to the starting fret required to play the scale you've selected in the same key.

3: For example, if you're playing the Phrygian #3 mode in the key of Emaj, we need to start it from the 4th fret. So even though the starting note here would be G#, not E, the combined notes in the completed scale are the same as those in the key of Emajor.

4: All the scales in each key will be the same, provided the starting fret for each scale lines up horizontally with the fret number to the left of it. For example, the key of Gm will have the following: Harmonic minor = fret 3, Locrian #6 = fret 5, Ionian #5 = fret 6, Dorian #4 = fret 8, Phrygian #3 = fret 10, Lydian #2 = fret 11 & the Mixolydian #1 = fret 2.

43: Basic Melodic minor theory:

Before you study this section, please make sure you have an understanding of the modes first!

43.1: Every major key has a **relative minor**, in other words a minor scale that contains the same notes as the major key it's related to, but simply starting on a different note. The minor scale starts on the **6th note** of the related major scale. We refer to this minor scale as the 'natural' minor. The natural minor's modal name is Aeolian.

43.2: Now we'll compare the Cmajor scale to the Aminor. (the A natural minor)

C T D T E S F T G T A T B S C = Cmaj scale
A T B S C T D T E S F T G T A = Amin scale

43.3: Now, we get 3 types of minor scales, let's compare them starting on the note A:

```
natural minor :  A  T  B  S  C  T  D  T  E  S  F  T  G  T  A
melodic minor :  A  T  B  S  C  T  D  T  E  T  F#  T  G#  S  A
harmonic minor :  A  T  B  S  C  T  D  T  E  S  F  1½  G#  S  A
```

43.4: The Melodic minor scale has **2 basic characteristics**, these are :
The Melodic minor does not ascend and descend with the same notes. It ascends with a raised 6 & 7th, but descends like the natural minor. Let's compare this starting on the note A.

```
A  T  B  S  C  T  D  T  E  T  F#  T  G#  S  A  T  G  T  F  S  E  T  D  T  C  S  B  T  A
|<      ascending as melodic minor, note #6 & 7      >|<      descending as the natural minor, no #'s!      >|
```

43.5: As with modes, we have 7 positions within the melodic minor scale, these are:
(*Please note that for comparison purposes only, we're going to compare to the A Melodic minor.*)

note positions:	1	2	3	4	5	6	7	8		1	2	3	4	5	6	7	8	note positions:
A Melodic Minor :	A	B	C	D	E	F#	G#	A		A	B	C	D	E	F	G	A	: A Natural Minor
B Dorian b2 :	B	C	D	E	F#	G#	A	B		B	C#	D	E	F#	G#	A	B	: B Dorian
C Lydian augmented :	C	D	E	F#	G#	A	B	C		C	D	E	F#	G	A	B	C	: C Lydian
D Lydian b7 :	D	E	F#	G#	A	B	C	D		D	E	F#	G#	A	B	C#	D	: D Lydian
E Mixolydian b6 :	E	F#	G#	A	B	C	D	E		E	F#	G#	A	B	C#	D	E	: E Mixolydian
F# Locrian #2 :	F#	G#	A	B	C	D	E	F#		F#	G	A	B	C	D	E	F#	: F# Locrian
G# Super Locrian :	G#	A	B	C	D	E	F#	G#		G#	A	B	C#	D	E	F#	G#	: G# Locrian

43.6: To appreciate the Melodic minor mode names, let's look at the notes in the B Dorian b2 mode and compare it to the standard B Dorian mode. We'll notice the 2nd note is a 'C' in the Dorian b2, while we have a C# in the standard B Dorian mode. Because we compare the Melodic minor modes to the standard modes, we now see the 2nd note of the Dorian b2 is flattened, and this is how it gets it's name.

43.7: The key to understanding how the Melodic modes get their names, is to compare it to the standard modes. We do this as the standard modes are all derived from positions on the Major scale, and we should know by now that the major scale is our reference for all scales.

43.8: **Basic triads in the key of A melodic minor:**

Please remember that triads are chords that have 3 different notes..

chords built with ascending notes :	Am	Bm	Caug	D	E	F#dim	G#dim
chords built with descending notes :	G	F	Em	Dm	C	Bdim	Am

43.9: This means we can expect to see a combination of both rows of the chords listed here! The sequence of the chords will depend on the melody, so if you're new to the melodic minor scale, rather consult with a music teacher as to the correct classical theory for some interesting insight to the application of the Melodic minor. Please keep in mind the purpose of this book is to provide you with a practical knowledge of chords and scale shapes, and how the relate to keys at a surface level.

44: The Melodic Minor scales:

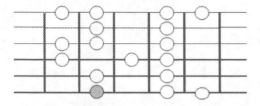

44.1: **The Melodic minor** is position 1. When comparing to the natural minor, please observe that the 6th &7th notes and their octaves are raised (#) for the Melodic minor. At fret 5 this is the A Melodic minor.

5	Cmaj/Amin	A Melodic
6	**C#maj/A#min**	**Bb Melodic**
7	Dmaj/Bmin	B Melodic
8	**Ebmaj/Cmin**	**C Melodic**
9	Emaj/C#min	C# Melodic
10	**Fmaj/Dmin**	**D Melodic**
11	F#maj/D#min	Eb Melodic
12	**Gmaj/Emin**	**E Melodic**
13	Abmaj/Fmin	F Melodic
2	**Amaj/F#mai**	**F# Melodic**
3	Bbmaj/Gmin	G Melodic
4	**Bmaj/G#min**	**G# Melodic**

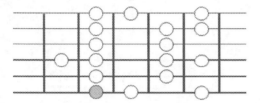

44.2: **The Dorian b2** is our 2nd mode. When comparing to this scale to the Dorian mode, please observe that the 2nd[h] note and its octaves are flattened (b). At fret 7 this is still in the key of Amin (Cmajor).

7	Cmaj/Amin	B Dorian b2
8	**C#maj/A#min**	**C Dorian b2**
9	Dmaj/Bmin	C# Dorian b2
10	**Ebmaj/Cmin**	**D Dorian b2**
11	Emaj/C#min	D# Dorian b2
12	**Fmaj/Dmin**	**E Dorian b2**
13	F#maj/D#min	F Dorian b2
2	**Gmaj/Emin**	**F# Dorian b2**
3	Abmaj/Fmin	G Dorian b2
4	**Amaj/F#mai**	**G# Dorian b2**
5	Bbmaj/Gmin	A Dorian b2
6	**Bmaj/G#min**	**A# Dorian b2**

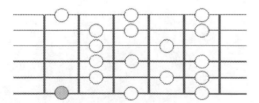

44.3: **The Lydian augmented** is our 3rd mode. The 4 tone intervals that begin this scale give it the augmented characteristic. If we're in Amin, this mode would start at fret 8.

8	Cmaj/Amin	C Lydian Aug
9	**C#maj/A#min**	**C# Lydian Aug**
10	Dmaj/Bmin	D Lydian Aug
11	**Ebmaj/Cmin**	**Eb Lydian Aug**
12	Emaj/C#min	E Lydian Aug
13	**Fmaj/Dmin**	**F Lydian Aug**
2	F#maj/D#min	F# Lydian Aug
3	**Gmaj/Emin**	**G Lydian Aug**
4	Abmaj/Fmin	Ab Lydian Aug
5	**Amaj/F#mai**	**A Lydian Aug**
6	Bbmaj/Gmin	Bb Lydian Aug
7	**Bmaj/G#min**	**B Lydian Aug**

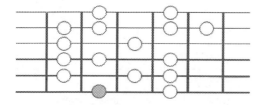

10	Cmaj/Amin	D Lydian b7
11	**C#maj/A#min**	**D# Lydian b7**
12	Dmaj/Bmin	**E Lydian b7**
13	**Ebmaj/Cmin**	F Lydian b7
2	Emaj/C#min	**F# Lydian b7**
3	**Fmaj/Dmin**	G Lydian b7
4	F#maj/D#min	**G# Lydian b7**
5	**Gmaj/Emin**	A Lydian b7
6	Abmaj/Fmin	**Bb Lydian b7**
7	**Amaj/F#mai**	B Lydian b7
8	Bbmaj/Gmin	**C Lydian b7**
9	**Bmaj/G#min**	C# Lydian b7

44.4: The Lydian b7, the 4th mode. Comparing this to the Lydian as found in unaltered scales we'd notice that the 7th note and it's octaves have been flattened.

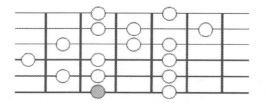

12	Cmaj/Amin	E Mixolydian b6
13	**C#maj/A#min**	**F Mixolydian b6**
2	Dmaj/Bmin	F# Mixolydian b6
3	**Ebmaj/Cmin**	**G Mixolydian b6**
4	Emaj/C#min	G# Mixolydian b6
5	**Fmaj/Dmin**	**A Mixolydian b6**
6	F#maj/D#min	A# Mixolydian b6
7	**Gmaj/Emin**	**B Mixolydian b6**
8	Abmaj/Fmin	C Mixolydian b6
9	**Amaj/F#mai**	**C# Mixolydian b6**
10	Bbmaj/Gmin	D Mixolydian b6
11	**Bmaj/G#min**	**D# Mixolydian b6**

44.5: The Mixolydian b6, another major related mode very similar to the standard Mixolydian, but the 6th note here (and it's octaves) have all been flattened.

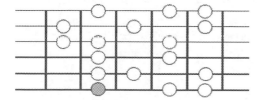

2	Cmaj/Amin	F# Locrian #2
3	**C#maj/A#min**	**G Locrian #2**
4	Dmaj/Bmin	G# Locrian #2
5	**Ebmaj/Cmin**	**A Locrian #2**
6	Emaj/C#min	A# Locrian #2
7	**Fmaj/Dmin**	**B Locrian #2**
8	F#maj/D#min	C Locrian #2
9	**Gmaj/Emin**	**C# Locrian #2**
10	Abmaj/Fmin	D Locrian #2
11	**Amaj/F#mai**	D# Locrian #2
12	Bbmaj/Gmin	E Locrian #2
13	**Bmaj/G#min**	**F Locrian #2**

44.6: The Locrian #2, we can build diminished chords from both positions 6 & 7 of the Melodic minor scale. This is justifies the Locrian #2 mode in this position.

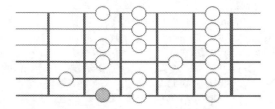

4	Cmaj/Amin	G# Super Locrian
5	**C#maj/A#min**	**A Locrian #2**
6	Dmaj/Bmin	A# Locrian #2
7	**Ebmaj/Cmin**	**B Locrian #2**
8	Emaj/C#min	C Locrian #2
9	**Fmaj/Dmin**	**C# Locrian #2**
10	F#maj/D#min	D Locrian #2
11	**Gmaj/Emin**	**D# Locrian #2**
12	Abmaj/Fmin	E Locrian #2
13	**Amaj/F#mai**	**F Locrian #2**
2	Bbmaj/Gmin	Gb Locrian #2
3	**Bmaj/G#min**	**G Locrian #2**

44.6: **The Super Locrian,** as mentioned, we can build diminished chord from both positions 6 & 7 of the Melodic minor scale.

Reading the Melodic scale charts.

1: The highlighted note is the starting note. The scale needs to begin on the fret number on the left!

2: The grid chart allows us to line up the key you need to the starting fret required to play the scale you've selected in the same key.

3: For example, if you're playing the Super Locrian mode in the key of Abmaj, we need to start it from the 12th fret. So even though the starting note here would be E, not Ab, the combined notes in the completed scale are as needed for the key of Abmajor.

4: All the scales in each key will be the same, provided the starting fret for each scale lines up horizontally with the fret number to the left of it. For example, the key of Gm will have the following: Melodic minor = fret 3, Dorian b2 = fret 5, Lydian Augmented = fret 6, Lydian b7 = fret 8, Mixolydian b6 = fret 10, Locrian #2 = fret 12 & the Super Locrian = fret 2.

45: A few useful exercises:

On this page I've listed some of my personal favorite exercises that I enjoy while improvising. They're designed to help our knowledge of the scales, and to add applications & techniques to them.

Ex1: - using the Pentatonic

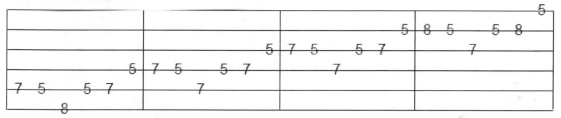

1a: This exercise uses triplets to work through position 1 of the minor pentatonic scale. Please first learn the riff picking all the notes, then try some hammer-ons & pull-offs on the strings that have 2 notes in a row.

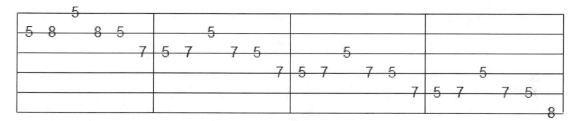

1b: The reverse of ex1a. Once more, first learn the exercise picking all the notes, then apply hammer-on's & pull-off's.

Ex2: - Joining the Modes

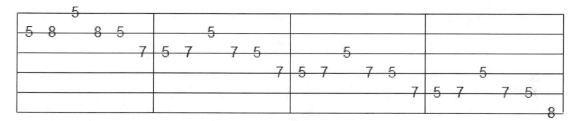

2: Unlike ex1 that works across the strings, this exercise uses all the frets. We've not included the descending TAB's, but please try reversing the exercise

Ex3: - Peddling

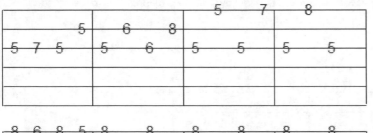

Ex3.1: We've taken the last 8 notes of the Aeolian mode, and simply played ascending. The key is to notice that every alternate note is the starting note. This technique is called peddling.

Ex3.2: This is the same concept as ex 3a, but descending. So this time the 'peddled' note is the highest pitched note, making it a great pinky exercise.

Ex4: - Ascending using the Ionian mode

With this exercise we need to notice that each triplet begins on the 2nd note of the previous triplet. Once you've mastered this, please revserse it.

Then, try and apply this concept to all the other modes, as well as any scale that you like, even the Pentatonic & Blues scales sound great with this exercise.

To get the best out of any exercise, play it at the lower frets, for example frets 3 or 5. Then play exactly the same exercise from fret 12. And, if your guitar allows, try it at fret 17 too. This will help get your fingers used to wide and narrow frets which essential for various keys.

Guitar playing is for enjoyment. So in the words of the legendary guitarist Frank Zappa " Shut up and play your guitar.."